Bridge: the golden principles

Jeremy Flint is World Master of the World Bridge Federation,
Grand Master of the English Bridge Union and Life Master of
the American Contract Bridge League. He has competed in
numerous international bridge tournaments and is the author of
six previous books on bridge. He is bridge correspondent of *The
Times* and has appeared, both as player and as commentator, in
the television series *Grand Slam* and *Bridge Club*, a series for
beginners.

Freddie North has won most of the major competitions in his
own country and is one of Great Britain's most successful rubber
bridge players. He represented Britain at the 1960 and 1964
World Pairs Olympiads and has played in many international
matches. He is a bridge and racing journalist. Principal of the
Sussex School of Bridge, he lives in Hove, Sussex.

The authors' companion volume, *Bridge: the first principles* – for
beginners – is also available from Pan Books.

Also by Jeremy Flint and Freddie North
in Pan Books

Bridge: the first principles

by Jeremy Flint and John Gullick

The First Bridge Book

JEREMY FLINT and
FREDDIE NORTH

Bridge:
the golden principles

Pan Original
Pan Books London and Sydney

First published 1985 by Pan Books Ltd,
Cavaye Place, London SW10 9PG
The section on dummy play was first published by
Zephyr House, Leatherhead as *Bridge: the golden principles
of dummy play* in different form in 1979
9 8 7 6 5 4 3 2 1
© Jeremy Flint and Freddie North 1979, 1985
ISBN 0 330 29000 2
Photoset by Parker Typesetting Service, Leicester
Printed and bound in Great Britain by
Cox & Wyman Ltd, Reading

Introduction

The transition from competent novice to accomplished card player is not nearly so difficult as some imagine. The essence of good dummy play is the recognition of the problem; the technique required to solve it is only secondary.

Obviously, until you are familiar with the various coups we describe, some hands will be beyond your scope. But despite their imposing names – end-plays, squeezes, precaution plays, etc. – they are mechanically undemanding.

Naturally we will describe the technique you require, but more importantly we will help you to see when you need to use your new-found knowledge.

When you play bridge there is no one to ring a bell to warn you that something difficult awaits. We reproduce that realistic setting, but amplify the value of the examples by extracting a *principle*. This principle will help you to spot the innumerable hands which demand similar technique when you see them again at the table. So on every right-hand page of this book you will find an example of a bridgehand which poses a question. On the next page you will find the answer, plus an explanation of the principle involved.

Defence poses problems of its own. We believe we can teach you to be a good defender. We can teach you to signal, to unravel declarer's plan – and then frustrate it. We can teach you to help your partner. But what about that partner? We know from bitter experience that defending with a stubborn or ignorant ally can be infuriating. Perhaps you can lend him this book, or in the last resort he might even go to the shops and . . .

We have deliberately constructed some examples which are similar, in order to illustrate a theme fully. These are not put next door to each other, because we hope that you will recognize the plays on the second occasion. If you fail, don't be discouraged. A brazil nut is not necessarily cracked with the first blow, or even the second.

Dummy play

The object of these fifty-two examples is to equip the reader with sufficient technical skill to handle the everyday problems of play. Those exotic coups that occur every blue moon have no place in this book because they would be of little practical benefit to the reader. Nevertheless, the range of subjects is sufficiently comprehensive to ensure that anyone who masters them can face his bridge friends, and especially his partner, with complete confidence.

Contents

1 Love all; dealer South. Contract: 4S by South.

♠ Q J 6 5
♡ 8 5 4 2
♢ A 9
♣ K 10 4

♠ A K 9 7 4 2
♡ 9 3
♢ J 10
♣ A J 3

The bidding

S	W	N	E
1♠	2♡	3♠	Pass
4♠	Pass	Pass	Pass

West plays three top hearts, East following to the first two rounds and then discarding the eight of diamonds. How should South plan the play?

Simple elimination

1 Love all; dealer South. Contract: 4S by South.

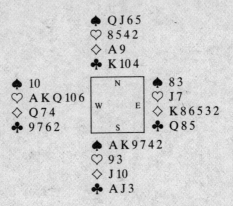

```
                    ♠ Q J 6 5
                    ♡ 8 5 4 2
                    ◇ A 9
                    ♣ K 10 4
    ♠ 10                          ♠ 8 3
    ♡ A K Q 10 6      N           ♡ J 7
    ◇ Q 7 4       W       E       ◇ K 8 6 5 3 2
    ♣ 9 7 6 2         S           ♣ Q 8 5
                    ♠ A K 9 7 4 2
                    ♡ 9 3
                    ◇ J 10
                    ♣ A J 3
```

The play
South should ruff the third heart, draw trumps, ruff the fourth heart and play the ace and another diamond. The opponent who wins the diamond trick will be faced with the unenviable choice of opening up the club suit or giving declarer a ruff and discard.

The principle
Taking all safe cards of exit away from the defenders leaves them with the choice of playing into declarer's danger suit – the suit that he does not wish to tackle himself – or conceding a ruff in one hand and a discard in the other.

2 Game all; dealer South. Contract: 3NT by South.

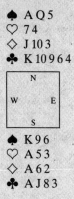

♠ A Q 5
♥ 7 4
♦ J 10 3
♣ K 10 9 6 4

♠ K 9 6
♥ A 5 3
♦ A 6 2
♣ A J 8 3

The bidding

S	W	N	E
1♣	1♥	3♣	Pass
3NT	Pass	Pass	Pass

West leads the king of hearts. How should South plan the play?

Hold up and safety play

2 Game all; dealer South. Contract: 3NT by South.

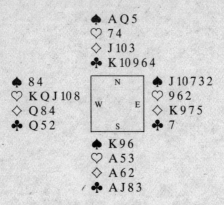

```
              ♠ A Q 5
              ♡ 7 4
              ♢ J 10 3
              ♣ K 10 9 6 4

  ♠ 8 4            N          ♠ J 10 7 3 2
  ♡ K Q J 10 8                ♡ 9 6 2
  ♢ Q 8 4      W       E      ♢ K 9 7 5
  ♣ Q 5 2          S          ♣ 7

              ♠ K 9 6
              ♡ A 5 3
              ♢ A 6 2
              ♣ A J 8 3
```

The play
South should withhold the ♡A until the third round. The ♣A
comes next followed by the ♣J. If West plays a low club on the
second round the finesse *must* be taken. South can afford to lose
a club to East but not to West.

The principle
The hold up is a common play, especially at no trumps. It is
designed to sever communication between the opponents.
Taking the club finesse through West is a safety play which
declarer can afford. Sometimes it will cost a trick. More important – it will always safeguard the contract.

3 Love all; dealer South. Contract: 3NT by South.

♠ K 10 5
♡ Q 10 9
◇ 8 2
♣ A J 10 9 7

♠ A Q J 3
♡ A J 8 5
◇ K J 4
♣ Q 8

The bidding

S	N
1♡	2♣
3NT	

West leads the five of diamonds, East contributing the queen. How should South plan the play and should his strategy alter if East were to play the ace of diamonds to the first trick and then continue the suit?

Taking the right finesse

3 Love all; dealer South. Contract: 3NT by South.

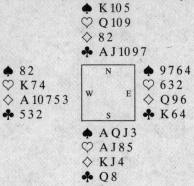

```
                 ♠ K 10 5
                 ♡ Q 10 9
                 ◇ 8 2
                 ♣ A J 10 9 7
   ♠ 8 2                          ♠ 9 7 6 4
   ♡ K 7 4              N         ♡ 6 3 2
   ◇ A 10 7 5 3    W        E     ◇ Q 9 6
   ♣ 5 3 2              S         ♣ K 6 4
                 ♠ A Q J 3
                 ♡ A J 8 5
                 ◇ K J 4
                 ♣ Q 8
```

The play

South should win East's ◇Q with the king, enter dummy with a spade and take the heart finesse. This plan will ensure at least nine tricks, even if the ♡K is wrong, as declarer's ◇J is protected while West is on lead. To take the club finesse would result in losing four diamonds and one club. Refusing the ◇Q would not help since West would duck the continuation.

If East holds the ◇A declarer adopts a different strategy. Suppose East wins the first trick with the ◇A and continues the suit, declarer should withold the ◇K until the third round and then play on clubs – not hearts. This plan will yield at least 4 spades, 1 heart, 1 diamond and 3 clubs.

The principle

Although it is usually right to play on the long suit when extra tricks have to be developed in no trumps, there are sometimes more important considerations. An urgent priority can be to protect some fragile holding, in this example the ◇J. Now one must look to a less promising suit for the extra tricks. Naturally, whichever suit one selects must be capable of providing sufficient tricks. In this case it is correct to play on hearts rather than clubs. But note how the plan should be amended if East produces the ◇A on the first round: now declarer must cut the communications, since it is West that has become the danger hand.

4 E-W game; dealer West. Contract: 4H by South.

♠ J 5 4
♡ J 9 7 5
♢ A 8
♣ K J 5 2

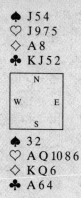

♠ 3 2
♡ A Q 10 8 6
♢ K Q 6
♣ A 6 4

The bidding

S	W	N	E
—	Pass	Pass	Pass
1♡	Pass	3♡	Pass
4♡	Pass	Pass	Pass

West starts the attack with ace, king and another spade, East playing the ten, eight and queen. South ruffs the third round of spades, enters dummy with the ace of diamonds and takes the heart finesse which loses to West. West exits with the knave of diamonds. How should South plan the play?

4 E-W game; dealer West. Contract: 4H by South.

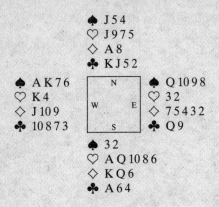

```
              ♠ J 5 4
              ♡ J 9 7 5
              ◇ A 8
              ♣ K J 5 2
  ♠ A K 7 6    ┌───────┐    ♠ Q 10 9 8
  ♡ K 4        │   N   │    ♡ 3 2
  ◇ J 10 9     │ W   E │    ◇ 7 5 4 3 2
  ♣ 10 8 7 3   │   S   │    ♣ Q 9
              └───────┘
              ♠ 3 2
              ♡ A Q 10 8 6
              ◇ K Q 6
              ♣ A 6 4
```

The play
South wins the diamond switch in hand, draws trumps and lays
down the ace and king of clubs. When the queen falls he is home.
Since West passed originally and has already turned up with
eleven points East *must* hold the ♣Q. It is therefore pointless to
finesse. The only hope is a doubleton queen.

The principle
When a finesse is doomed, which is usually determined by the
bidding and foregoing play, look for another line. In this
instance the doubleton queen with East is the only real chance.
Slender though it may appear, it is better than no chance at all.

5 Game all; dealer South. Contract: 4S by South.

♠ 9 5 2
♡ 6 3 2
♢ A K 5
♣ A K 5 2

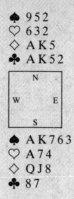

♠ A K 7 6 3
♡ A 7 4
♢ Q J 8
♣ 8 7

The bidding

S	N
1♠	2♣
2♠	4♠

West leads the king of hearts which South wins with the ace. South now lays down the ace and king of spades, but on the second round West shows out, discarding the three of clubs. How should South plan the play?

Coup en passant

5 Game all; dealer South. Contract: 4S by South.

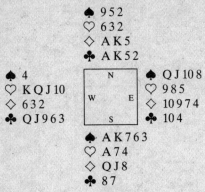

♠ 9 5 2
♡ 6 3 2
◇ A K 5
♣ A K 5 2

♠ 4
♡ K Q J 10
◇ 6 3 2
♣ Q J 9 6 3

♠ Q J 10 8
♡ 9 8 5
◇ 10 9 7 4
♣ 10 4

♠ A K 7 6 3
♡ A 7 4
◇ Q J 8
♣ 8 7

The play

Declarer should cash the ♣AK and ruff a club. He now plays three rounds of diamonds, finishing in dummy, which leaves the following position:

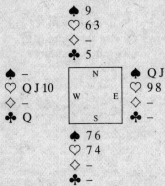

♠ 9
♡ 6 3
◇ –
♣ 5

♠ –
♡ Q J 10
◇ –
♣ Q

♠ Q J
♡ 9 8
◇ –
♣ –

♠ 7 6
♡ 7 4
◇ –
♣ –

If East had the lead at this point he could soon polish off the remainder of the tricks. However, the lead is with dummy and declarer plays the ♣5. Now South must score one more spade trick for his contract *en passant*.

The principle

The name of this coup, which means, literally, a blow in passing, is taken from chess. It is a play that enables declarer to make a low trump when it is situated over a defender's higher trump. Although in the hand above it seems that South must lose two spades and two hearts, one loser disappears as he plays dummy's last club. The time to look for this play is when you cannot draw all the outstanding trumps, or do not wish to, and have cards to ruff that can be played through the defender with the recalcitrant trump holding.

*

6 N-S game; dealer South. Contract: 3NT by South.

♠ Q 2
♡ K 6 2
♢ A Q J 8 4
♣ 8 6 4

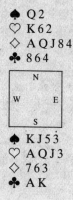

♠ K J 5 3
♡ A Q J 3
♢ 7 6 3
♣ A K

The bidding:

S	N
1♡	2♢
3NT	

West leads the queen of clubs. How should South plan the play?

19

Counting the tricks

6 N-S game; dealer South. Contract: 3NT by South.

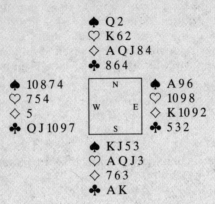

♠ Q 2
♡ K 6 2
♢ A Q J 8 4
♣ 8 6 4

♠ 10 8 7 4
♡ 7 5 4
♢ 5
♣ Q J 10 9 7

♠ A 9 6
♡ 10 9 8
♢ K 10 9 2
♣ 5 3 2

♠ K J 5 3
♡ A Q J 3
♢ 7 6 3
♣ A K

The play
Declarer should resist the temptation of taking the diamond
finesse at trick two. If it loses and the diamonds fail to break
eight tricks will prove the limit. On the other hand, a spade at
trick two will ensure nine tricks.

The principle
It is always imperative to count the winners before deciding upon
your plan. In this case nine tricks are certain providing you play a
spade at trick two. If you attack diamonds you will be held to
eight tricks since East will surely remove your last club control.
Although it is usually right to develop the longest suit, counting
your tricks will show you when to look elsewhere.

7 Game all; dealer North. Contract: 4S by South.

♠ 7 5 4 3
♡ 9 2
♢ A 5 3
♣ A J 10 6

♠ A K Q J 10 9
♡ J 4 3
♢ K 6 2
♣ 4

The bidding

S	W	N	E
—	—	Pass	Pass
1♠	2♡	3♠	Pass
4♠	Pass	Pass	Pass

West leads the two top hearts, East playing the seven and then the five. West continues with the queen of hearts. How should South plan the play?

Loser on loser

7 Game all; dealer North. Contract: 4S by South.

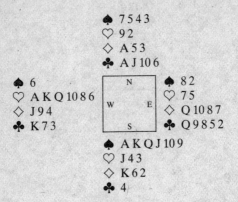

♠ 7543
♡ 92
◇ A53
♣ AJ106

♠ 6
♡ AKQ1086
◇ J94
♣ K73

♠ 82
♡ 75
◇ Q1087
♣ Q9852

♠ AKQJ109
♡ J43
◇ K62
♣ 4

The play

With nine tricks on top South needs a ruff in dummy for his tenth trick. However, it would be foolish to try to ruff a heart since there is a grave risk that East will overruff – as would happen in practice. A much safer plan is to discard a diamond from dummy. Then, when declarer wins the lead, he can draw trumps and ruff a diamond without risk.

The principle

When you need one extra trick via a ruff it is not always obligatory to ruff what is offered to you. By doing a straight swop – i.e. discarding a loser on a loser – it is often possible to take a safe ruff rather than a dangerous one.

8 E-W game; dealer East. Contract: 4H by South.

> ♠ A K
> ♡ J 10 8 7 5 3
> ♢ Q 4 3
> ♣ J 7

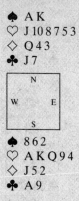

> ♠ 8 6 2
> ♡ A K Q 9 4
> ♢ J 5 2
> ♣ A 9

The bidding

S	W	N	E
—	—	—	Pass
1♡	1♠	4♡	Pass
Pass	Pass		

West leads the king of clubs. How should South plan the play?

Simple elimination

8 E-W game; dealer East. Contract: 4H by South.

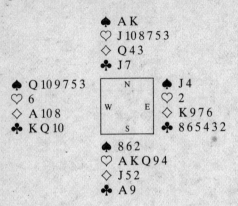

```
                    ♠ A K
                    ♡ J 10 8 7 5 3
                    ♢ Q 4 3
                    ♣ J 7
 ♠ Q 10 9 7 5 3          N            ♠ J 4
 ♡ 6                                  ♡ 2
 ♢ A 10 8         W          E        ♢ K 9 7 6
 ♣ K Q 10               S             ♣ 8 6 5 4 3 2
                    ♠ 8 6 2
                    ♡ A K Q 9 4
                    ♢ J 5 2
                    ♣ A 9
```

The play

With nine tricks on top declarer requires one more. He should win the opening lead with the ♣A, draw trumps, cash the ♠AK, re-enter his hand with a trump and ruff his last spade. The time is now right to exit with ♣J. The defence may cash ♢AK, providing declarer with his tenth trick, or concede a ruff and discard which will do just as well.

The principle

By stripping the opponents of their safe cards of exit, declarer can dispose of the lead at a time when the defence are forced to open up a suit to his advantage (in this instance diamonds) or concede a ruff and discard.

9 Game all; dealer South. Contract: 5D by South.

♠ A 6 2
♡ 6 3
◇ Q 10 7 5
♣ K 6 5 3

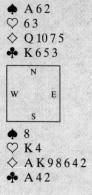

♠ 8
♡ K 4
◇ A K 9 8 6 4 2
♣ A 4 2

The bidding

S	W	N	E
1◇	Double	3◇	3♠
5◇	Pass	Pass	Pass

West leads the king of spades. How should South plan the play?

Avoidance play

9 Game all; dealer South. Contract: 5D by South.

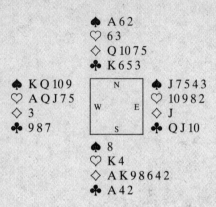

```
              ♠ A 6 2
              ♡ 6 3
              ◇ Q 10 7 5
              ♣ K 6 5 3
♠ K Q 10 9        N        ♠ J 7 5 4 3
♡ A Q J 7 5              ♡ 10 9 8 2
◇ 3         W       E     ◇ J
♣ 9 8 7           S       ♣ Q J 10
              ♠ 8
              ♡ K 4
              ◇ A K 9 8 6 4 2
              ♣ A 4 2
```

The play
With ten tricks on top declarer needs to make one more from either hearts or clubs. His best play is to duck the ♠K. Let us suppose West continues with the ♠Q. Dummy wins the ace while South discards the ♣2. Declarer draws trumps and can test the clubs in perfect safety, cashing the ace and king and ruffing the third round. The thirteenth club is now established for the vital discard. In all declarer makes 7 diamonds, 3 clubs and 1 spade.

The principle
The bidding suggests that the ♡A will be with West, so declarer should be reluctant to pin his hopes on making a trick from this suit. In any case first he must try to establish the fourth club for a discard. The snag is that East may win and switch to a heart. This kind of problem can often be resolved by arranging to lose a trick in another suit rather than in the vital one. The advantage of this transposition is clearly illustrated above where the danger hand is prevented from obtaining the lead.

10 Game all; dealer South. Contract: 3NT by South.

♠ J 7
♡ A 7 5 3
♢ 9 2
♣ A Q 10 9 5

♠ A K 5 4 3
♡ K 6
♢ A J 3
♣ J 8 2

The bidding

S	N
1♠	2♣
2NT	2NT

West leads the five of diamonds, East contributing the queen. How should South plan the play?

Hold up

10 Game all; dealer South. Contract: 3NT by South.

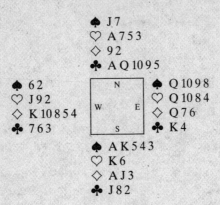

```
              ♠ J 7
              ♡ A 7 5 3
              ◇ 9 2
              ♣ A Q 10 9 5
♠ 6 2                         ♠ Q 10 9 8
♡ J 9 2         N            ♡ Q 10 8 4
◇ K 10 8 5 4  W   E          ◇ Q 7 6
♣ 7 6 3          S           ♣ K 4
              ♠ A K 5 4 3
              ♡ K 6
              ◇ A J 3
              ♣ J 8 2
```

The play
Declarer should refuse the first diamond trick, and if the suit is continued he must refuse the second round also. Winning trick three, he takes the losing club finesse but still makes nine tricks with 4 clubs, 1 diamond, 2 hearts and 2 spades.

The principle
Whether declarer should win the first trick or not may be decided by the manner in which he will have to play any other critical suit. In this case he must play on clubs and finesse into the East hand. For that reason it is necessary to break up the diamond communication. Suppose the spades were stronger and declarer had to finesse into the West hand, now he would win the first diamond trick so that the knave of diamonds was still protected.

11 Game all; dealer South. Contract: 6NT by South.

♠ A K 6 4
♥ 8 7 4
♦ 9 8
♣ A 7 5 2

♠ Q 7
♥ A 5 3
♦ A K Q J 10
♣ K 6 3

The bidding

S	N
1♦	1♠
3NT	4NT
6♦	6NT

North left nothing unbid with his quantitative try of four no trumps. South decided that his solid suit was sufficient reason to bid the slam and gave his partner the choice between diamonds and no trumps. West led the king of hearts. How should South plan the play?

Simple squeeze

11 Game all; dealer South. Contract: 6NT by South.

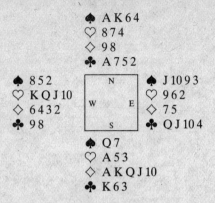

```
          ♠ A K 6 4
          ♡ 8 7 4
          ◇ 9 8
          ♣ A 7 5 2
♠ 8 5 2        N        ♠ J 10 9 3
♡ K Q J 10             ♡ 9 6 2
◇ 6 4 3 2   W    E     ◇ 7 5
♣ 9 8          S        ♣ Q J 10 4
          ♠ Q 7
          ♡ A 5 3
          ◇ A K Q J 10
          ♣ K 6 3
```

The play

Declarer should duck the first round of hearts and win the continuation. He should then cash his five diamond winners. Before the last diamond is played this will be the position:

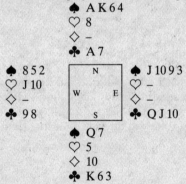

```
          ♠ A K 6 4
          ♡ 8
          ◇ –
          ♣ A 7
♠ 8 5 2        N        ♠ J 10 9 3
♡ J 10                 ♡ –
◇ –         W    E     ◇ –
♣ 9 8          S        ♣ Q J 10
          ♠ Q 7
          ♡ 5
          ◇ 10
          ♣ K 6 3
```

On the ◇10 West has no problem, dummy discards ♡8, but East is in grave trouble. If he parts with a spade, dummy's long spade becomes good. If he lets go a club, South's third club becomes established.

The principle

When one player has the task of guarding two suits (here it is East) it may be possible to exert pressure on him by playing off

30

the winners in your long suit. This pressure may force him to relinquish one of his guards. When playing for a squeeze, attempt to lose any trick that has to be lost at once so that the vice bites. This is known as 'rectifying the count'. Note, if South fails to duck the first heart East will not be embarrassed and the slam will fail. Remember, no matter how small a card may be it can become a menace, or threat card, should only one defender guard that suit.

*

12 E-W game; dealer West. Contract: 4H by South.

♠ 9 7 4
♡ 8 7 4
♢ A K 7
♣ A J 10 9

♠ 5 2
♡ A Q 6 5 2
♢ Q 10 9
♣ K Q 8

The bidding

S	W	N	E
—	1♠	Pass	Pass
Double	Pass	2♣	Pass
3♡	Pass	4♡	Pass
Pass	Pass		

West plays the ace, king and knave of spades, East following with the three and then the queen and discarding the two of diamonds on the third round. How should South plan the play?

12 E-W game; dealer West. Contract: 4H by South.

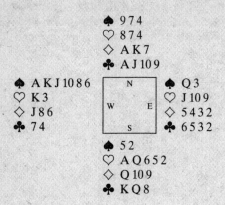

```
                    ♠ 9 7 4
                    ♡ 8 7 4
                    ◇ A K 7
                    ♣ A J 10 9
    ♠ A K J 10 8 6                   ♠ Q 3
    ♡ K 3                            ♡ J 10 9
    ◇ J 8 6                          ◇ 5 4 3 2
    ♣ 7 4                            ♣ 6 5 3 2
                    ♠ 5 2
                    ♡ A Q 6 5 2
                    ◇ Q 10 9
                    ♣ K Q 8
```

The play
South should ruff the third round of spades and play the ♡A
followed by a low heart. He will now lose only two spades and
one heart. The bidding makes it obvious that West holds the ♡K
so the finesse must be a losing play.

The principle
When the bidding makes it clear that a key card is misplaced,
declarer should look for other ways to succeed rather than take a
certain losing finesse. Since West is marked with the ♡K, (a) on
his opening bid and (b) on East's inability to respond, declarer's
only hope is to find West with Kx.

13 Game all; dealer South. Contract: 3NT by South.

♠ 6 5
♥ 3 2
♦ A K J 7 5 4 2
♣ 3 2

♠ A J 10
♥ A K 10
♦ 6 3
♣ A J 9 8 4

The bidding

S	N
1♣	1♦
2NT	3NT

West leads the four of spades, East contributing the queen. When South plays a diamond West follows with the eight. How should declarer plan the play?

Communication – safety play

13 Game all; dealer South. Contract: 3NT by South.

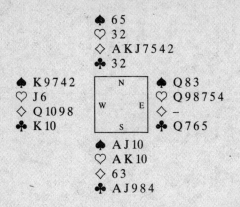

```
                    ♠ 6 5
                    ♡ 3 2
                    ♢ A K J 7 5 4 2
                    ♣ 3 2
    ♠ K 9 7 4 2                    ♠ Q 8 3
    ♡ J 6          N               ♡ Q 9 8 7 5 4
    ♢ Q 10 9 8   W   E             ♢ –
    ♣ K 10         S               ♣ Q 7 6 5
                    ♠ A J 10
                    ♡ A K 10
                    ♢ 6 3
                    ♣ A J 9 8 4
```

The play

Winning the first trick with the ♣A, declarer will naturally turn his attention to diamonds. Not requiring all seven tricks from the suit he need only concern himself with the possibility of a void. Declarer should, therefore, play a low diamond from dummy on West's eight! When East shows out the rest is plain sailing – as indeed would be the case if East followed suit. The subsequent diamond finesse will ensure six winners in this suit and a grand total of ten or eleven tricks in all.

The principle

When there is a long suit available for discards in one hand but entries are scarce, it is wise to look for a sure means of maintaining communication. If this entails conceding an extra trick, which you can afford, do not be mean about paying the small premium. After all, some insurance policies can be sound business.

Note that should West try the well known gambit of putting in the ♢Q on the first round, South should refuse to bite. He must duck and make certain of six tricks.

14 E-W game; dealer East. Contract: 4H by South.

♠ Q 10
♡ K 10 8 4
♢ A 8 5 2
♣ K 8 7

♠ J
♡ A Q J 9 7 6
♢ K Q 3
♣ 5 4 2

The bidding

S	W	N	E
—	—	—	1♠
2♡	Pass	3♡	Pass
4♡	Pass	Pass	Pass

West leads the three of spades. East wins with the king and then plays the ace. How should South plan the play?

Loser on loser

14 E-W game; dealer East. Contract: 4H by South.

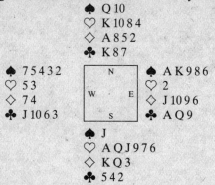

♠ Q 10
♡ K 10 8 4
♢ A 8 5 2
♣ K 8 7

♠ 7 5 4 3 2
♡ 5 3
♢ 7 4
♣ J 10 6 3

♠ A K 9 8 6
♡ 2
♢ J 10 9 6
♣ A Q 9

♠ J
♡ A Q J 9 7 6
♢ K Q 3
♣ 5 4 2

The play

There are nine tricks on top. A 3-3 diamond break or the ♣A with West would see declarer home, although both chances are against the odds: diamonds are more likely to divide 4-2 (48%) than 3-3 (36%) and the ♣A is more likely to be with East because of the opening bid. South should ruff the second spade, draw trumps and test the diamonds. When East shows up with four, declarer should allow him to hold the fourth diamond, discarding a losing club from hand. East will now have to concede the tenth trick either by playing a club or by giving a ruff and discard.

If West turns up with four diamonds, declarer should ruff the fourth round and play a club towards dummy. Maybe West will play low in which case the ♣7 will leave East on lead. Finally, if West plays a high club declarer's best chance is to duck on the first round but contribute the king on the club continuation. This succeeds when East has ♣Ax.

The principle

When one small card is a certain loser, no matter how declarer plays, it is good tactics to see if it can be lost to advantage. In this instance by discarding an inevitable club loser on the fourth diamond South ensures that his ♣K is protected while at the same time East is left without a safe card of exit.

15 E-W game; dealer West. Contract: 5D doubled by South.

♠ 5
♡ 8 3
♢ Q 10 8 4 2
♣ A K 8 7 3

♠ A 10 8 6 3
♡ A 9
♢ J 9 7 6
♣ Q 5

The bidding

S	W	N	E
—	1♡	2NT*	3♡
5♢	Pass	Pass	Double
Pass	Pass	Pass	

(*Showing the minors)

West leads the king of hearts. South wins with the ace and attempts to cash three rounds of clubs, but East ruffs the third round with the five of diamonds. How should declarer plan the play?

Crashing the trump honours

15 E-W game; dealer West. Contract: 5D doubled by South.

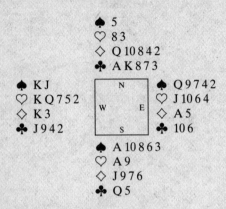

```
              ♠ 5
              ♡ 83
              ♢ Q 10 8 4 2
              ♣ A K 8 7 3
  ♠ K J          N          ♠ Q 9 7 4 2
  ♡ K Q 7 5 2               ♡ J 10 6 4
  ♢ K 3      W       E      ♢ A 5
  ♣ J 9 4 2      S          ♣ 10 6
              ♠ A 10 8 6 3
              ♡ A 9
              ♢ J 9 7 6
              ♣ Q 5
```

The play
South should overruff, play the ♠A and ruff a spade, ruff a club and ruff a second spade. Now dummy's master ♣8 is played. There is no point in East ruffing it with the ♢A so both he and South discard hearts. West takes this trick with the ♢3 and plays a heart which South ruffs. A trump lead now crashes the ace and king together.

The principle
When denied an early discard by an opponent ruffing one of your winners, you may recover by persevering with the suit. If the opponent's trumps are benignly distributed you can conclude by crashing their honours together.

16 Love all; dealer East. Contract: 6H by South.

♠ 9 7 6 3
♡ K 9 2
◇ A Q 10
♣ A K 5

♠ J
♡ A Q J 10 6
◇ K J 9 8
♣ 7 4 2

The bidding

S	W	N	E
—	—	—	Pass
1♡	1♠	3♣	Pass
3◇	Pass	3♡	Pass
4♡	Pass	5♣	Pass
6♡	Pass	Pass	Pass

An aggressive bidding sequence lands South in a small slam.
West starts with the ace and king of spades. How should South
plan the play?

Dummy reversal

16 Love all; dealer East. Contract: 6H by South.

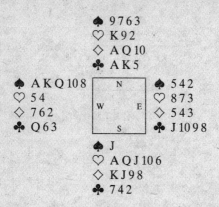

♠ 9763
♡ K92
◇ AQ10
♣ AK5

♠ AKQ108　　♠ 542
♡ 54　　　　　♡ 873
◇ 762　　　　◇ 543
♣ Q63　　　　♣ J1098

♠ J
♡ AQJ106
◇ KJ98
♣ 742

The play

Declarer ruffs the second spade with the ♡10, cashes, the ♡A and enters dummy with ♡9. A spade ruff and a club to dummy's ace are followed by a final spade ruff. Now dummy is re-entered with a diamond to draw the remaining trump, on which South discards his losing club.

The principle

When you are unable to make extra tricks by ruffing in dummy you can sometimes derive an advantage by taking ruffs in your own hand. The advantage occurs when dummy is left with more trumps than declarer. This process is known as 'Reversing the Dummy'. The signs for which to look are these: **1** Dummy's trumps, perhaps with the help of one top one from declarer, must be good enough to draw the outstanding trumps. **2** Declarer must have a shortage in his own hand to make ruffing possible. **3** There must be sufficient entries in dummy (a) to obtain the necessary number of ruffs and (b) to enter dummy eventually to extract the outstanding trump(s).

17 Game all; dealer East. Contract: 4S by South.

♠ A Q 10 4
♡ A 4
♢ 10 6 3
♣ K Q J 2

♠ J 9 8 7 2
♡ K 8 3
♢ K 5
♣ 9 8 4

The bidding

S	W	N	E
—	—	—	1♡
Pass	Pass	Double	Pass
1♠	Pass	2♠	Pass
2NT	Pass	4♠	Pass
Pass	Pass		

West leads the nine of hearts. How should declarer plan the play?

Remember the bidding

17 Game all; dealer East. Contract: 4S by South.

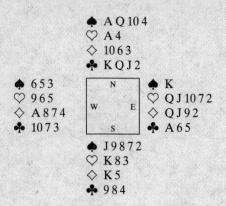

```
              ♠ A Q 10 4
              ♡ A 4
              ◇ 10 6 3
              ♣ K Q J 2
♠ 6 5 3              ♠ K
♡ 9 6 5        N     ♡ Q J 10 7 2
◇ A 8 7 4   W     E  ◇ Q J 9 2
♣ 10 7 3       S     ♣ A 6 5
              ♠ J 9 8 7 2
              ♡ K 8 3
              ◇ K 5
              ♣ 9 8 4
```

The play
Declarer should win the heart lead in hand and try the ♠J.
When West plays low, he rises with dummy's ace, no doubt
much to East's disappointment. Later he loses a club and two
diamonds, making exactly ten tricks.

The principle
On this occasion there are two critical cards to consider, the ◇A
and the ♠K. Bearing in mind West's original pass it is inconceivable that he will have both. If he has the ◇A and East the
guarded ♠K there is nothing to be done. Note that where you
lose a trick by rejecting the finesse it will be immaterial as East
will surely have the ◇A and your ◇K will score. The opportunities to utilize this type of hypothesis occur frequently. When
the opening bid has been passed make a note to consider the
maximum holding consistent with that pass.

18 E-W game; dealer West. Contract: 4S doubled by South.

♠ J 8 5
♥ A 6 2
♦ K 9 8
♣ K 10 9 5

♠ Q 10 9 7 6 2
♥ 7 3
♦ –
♣ A Q J 7 4

The bidding:

S	W	N	E
—	1♥	Pass	2♥
2♠	3♦	3♠	Pass
4♠	Double	Pass	Pass
Pass			

West leads the two of clubs. South wins in hand and plays a spade towards dummy. West wins with the king and switches to the four of hearts. How should declarer plan the play?

18 E-W game; dealer West. Contract: 4S doubled by South.

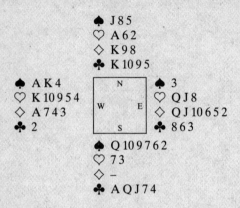

♠ J 8 5
♥ A 6 2
♦ K 9 8
♣ K 10 9 5

♠ A K 4
♥ K 10 9 5 4
♦ A 7 4 3
♣ 2

♠ 3
♥ Q J 8
♦ Q J 10 6 5 2
♣ 8 6 3

♠ Q 10 9 7 6 2
♥ 7 3
♦ –
♣ A Q J 7 4

The play
Declarer should win trick three with the ♥A and play the ♦K. When East follows with a small diamond, South discards his last heart. All enemy lines of communication are now cut, and it only remains for South to knock out the ♠A and draw the last trump.

The principle
West's lead is obviously a singleton so the danger is that the defence may take 2 spades, 1 heart and 1 ruff. However, in order to obtain the ruff, access to the East hand is required. When declarer is faced with this situation he must look for a way to cut the communications (that is why this play is called the 'scissors coup'). All that means is that you swop losers – but the safe hand is left on play.

19 E-W game; dealer East. Contract: 4H by South.

♠ A J 9
♡ 7 5 4 2
♢ K 2
♣ A K Q 2

♠ Q 5
♡ K Q J 10 9 8
♢ J 9
♣ 9 4 3

The bidding

S	W	N	E
—	—	—	1♢
1♡	Pass	4♡	Pass
Pass	Pass		

West leads the six of diamonds, dummy plays low and East wins the queen. East cashes the ace of diamonds and ace of hearts and exits with the knave of clubs. How should South plan the play?

45

Vienna coup

19 E-W game; dealer East. Contract: 4H by South.

```
                    ♠ A J 9
                    ♡ 7 5 4 2
                    ◇ K 2
                    ♣ A K Q 2
♠ 10 6 4 3 2          N          ♠ K 8 7
♡ 6 3                            ♡ A
◇ 6 5 4 3       W         E      ◇ A Q 10 8 7
♣ 6 5                S           ♣ J 10 8 7
                    ♠ Q 5
                    ♡ K Q J 10 9 8
                    ◇ J 9
                    ♣ 9 4 3
```

The play

There are nine tricks on top and declarer knows the contract will
succeed if the ♠K is with West, of if the clubs divide 3-3.
However, East is likely to hold the ♠K, in view of his opening
bid, and the chance of the clubs dividing evenly will not run
away, but if East has four clubs South must rely on a squeeze.
Trick four is won with the ♣Q and declarer continues with the
♡K, the ♣A, the ♠A and three more hearts, leaving the
following position:

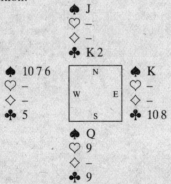

```
                    ♠ J
                    ♡ –
                    ◇ –
                    ♣ K 2
♠ 10 7 6             N          ♠ K
♡ –                             ♡ –
◇ –             W         E     ◇ –
♣ 5                  S          ♣ 10 8
                    ♠ Q
                    ♡ 9
                    ◇ –
                    ♣ 9
```

South plays the ♡9, dummy discards the ♠J and East is
squeezed. If he lets go a club, dummy's ♣2 becomes good. If he
parts with the ♠K, then declarer's ♠Q takes the next trick.

The principle
The essence of the Vienna coup is the temporary establishment of an opponent's card to master rank. The purpose is to ensure that your side is not squeezed rather than the defenders. Note that if the declarer had previously failed to cash the ♠A early on each player would have held one more spade in the end-game. Then, when the ♡9 is played, dummy is squeezed before East.

*

20 Love all; dealer South. Contract: 3NT by South.

♠ K 6 3
♡ Q J 6
♢ K J 9 8
♣ 8 7 6

♠ A 7 2
♡ A 4 2
♢ Q 10 7 6
♣ A J 10

The bidding:

S	N
1♢	3♢
3NT	

West leads the five of hearts, dummy's queen holding the trick. How should South plan the play?

Timing

20 Love all; dealer South. Contract: 3NT by South.

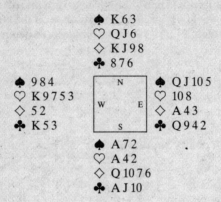

```
              ♠ K63
              ♡ QJ6
              ◇ KJ98
              ♣ 876
  ♠ 984                    ♠ QJ105
  ♡ K9753      N           ♡ 108
  ◇ 52       W   E         ◇ A43
  ♣ K53        S           ♣ Q942
              ♠ A72
              ♡ A42
              ◇ Q1076
              ♣ AJ10
```

The play
Declarer should lead a club from dummy at trick two, putting in
the ten when East plays low. West cannot profitably continue
hearts so will have to switch his attack. Whatever he plays
declarer should knock out the ◇A and subsequently take a
repeat finesse in clubs for his contract.

The principle
In order to establish his tricks declarer may be forced to relinquish the lead. When this is the case you must try to ensure that
it is only the innocuous opponent who obtains the lead in the first
instance. In the above example, if declarer makes the mistake of
knocking out the ◇A before playing on clubs East will win and
clear the heart suit. When West gets in with the ♣K he will then
cash the setting trick.

21 Game all; dealer South. Contract: 6NT by South.

           ♠ A J 10
           ♡ 10 6 3
           ♢ Q 9 5 4
           ♣ A Q 9

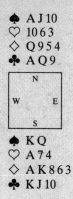

           ♠ K Q
           ♡ A 7 4
           ♢ A K 8 6 3
           ♣ K J 10

The bidding

      S   **N**
      2NT   6NT

West leads the king of hearts. How should South plan the play?

Precaution play

21 Game all; dealer South. Contract: 6NT by South.

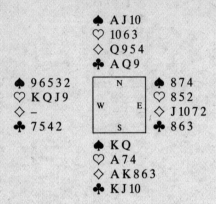

```
              ♠ A J 10
              ♡ 10 6 3
              ◇ Q 9 5 4
              ♣ A Q 9
♠ 9 6 5 3 2        N        ♠ 8 7 4
♡ K Q J 9                   ♡ 8 5 2
◇ –           W       E     ◇ J 10 7 2
♣ 7 5 4 2          S        ♣ 8 6 3
              ♠ K Q
              ♡ A 7 4
              ◇ A K 8 6 3
              ♣ K J 10
```

The play
Since there are twelve tricks on top providing the diamonds
divide no worse than 3-1, South should direct his attention to the
possibility of a 4-0 break. If West holds them all nothing can be
done, but if East is the custodian the suit can be picked up
without loss – providing declarer plays low to the queen before
touching a top honour from his own hand. The play goes: ♡A, a
low diamond to the queen and a diamond back towards the
closed hand, covering whatever East plays. Dummy is re-entered
with a black suit winner to pick up the rest of the diamonds.

The principle
When a contract depends on one isolated feature (in this case the
division of the diamond suit) you must concentrate on what *can*
be done to counter any adverse distribution.

22 E-W game; dealer West. Contract: 4H doubled by South.

♠ A 10 4
♡ K 7 3
◇ 10 9 8 6
♣ 7 6 4

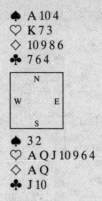

♠ 3 2
♡ A Q J 10 9 6 4
◇ A Q
♣ J 10

The bidding

S	W	N	E
—	2♠*	Pass	2NT§
3♡	3♠	4♡	Pass
Pass	Double	Pass	Pass
Pass			

(*A strong hand with a powerful
suit.)
(§The negative reply.)

West cashes the ace and king of clubs and then switches to the
king of spades. How should South plan the play?

Throw-in

22 E-W game; dealer West. Contract: 4H doubled by South.

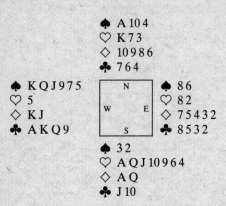

♠ A 10 4
♡ K 7 3
◇ 10 9 8 6
♣ 7 6 4

♠ K Q J 9 7 5   N   ♠ 8 6
♡ 5   W   E   ♡ 8 2
◇ K J   S   ◇ 7 5 4 3 2
♣ A K Q 9   ♣ 8 5 3 2

♠ 3 2
♡ A Q J 10 9 6 4
◇ A Q
♣ J 10

The play
With the ◇K almost certainly wrong, declarer must plan to throw West on lead so that he has to play a diamond up to South's AQ. Winning trick three with the ♠A, declarer cashes all the trumps so that his last three cards are ♠3, ◇AQ. West's last three cards – unless he has blanked the ◇K – will be ♠Q; ◇KJ. The ♠3 now forces West to lead a diamond.

The principle
It is futile to take a finesse which is virtually certain to lose. Strong bidding by a vulnerable opponent often suggests that he holds all the critical cards (including on this hand the ◇K). Visualize your own hand reduced to the essentials (in this case just three cards) and then try to imagine the three cards that your opponent must keep. Once you have done that the throw-in play becomes obvious.

23 Love all; dealer South. Contract: 4S by South.

$\spadesuit$ 10 7 6
$\heartsuit$ 10 9 8
$\diamondsuit$ 10 8 6 5 3
$\clubsuit$ J 3

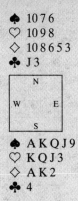

$\spadesuit$ A K Q J 9
$\heartsuit$ K Q J 3
$\diamondsuit$ A K 2
$\clubsuit$ 4

The bidding

S	N
2$\clubsuit$	2$\diamondsuit$
2$\spadesuit$	2NT
3$\heartsuit$	3$\spadesuit$
4$\clubsuit$	

West leads the ace of clubs and continues with the king of clubs. How should South plan the play?

Trump control

23 Love all; dealer South. Contract: 4S by South.

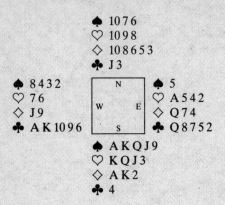

♠ 1076
♡ 1098
◇ 108653
♣ J3

♠ 8432
♡ 76
◇ J9
♣ A K 1096

♠ 5
♡ A542
◇ Q74
♣ Q8752

♠ AKQJ9
♡ KQJ3
◇ AK2
♣ 4

The play
South should refrain from ruffing the second club, discarding a diamond instead. Whatever the continuation, South draws trumps and loses only one more trick to the ace of hearts. If the defence play a third round of clubs the ruff is taken in dummy.

South will be defeated if he makes the mistake of ruffing at trick two. When he notes the bad trump break he will doubtless turn to hearts, but if East withholds his ace South can no longer maintain control.

The principle
The contract appears impregnable. On closer analysis the 4-1 trump break will defeat declarer if he grabs the second trick. Whenever there is a danger of losing trump control consider the possibility of postponing the ruff which shortens your trumps.

24 Game all; dealer South. Contract: 6C by South.

♠ J 10 6
♡ Q J 10 9
♢ A K
♣ A Q 8 6

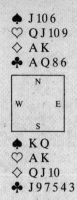

♠ K Q
♡ A K
♢ Q J 10
♣ J 9 7 5 4 3

The bidding

S	N
1♣	1♡
2NT	3♣
3♡	4♢
4♠	6♣

West leads the ace and another spade. How should South plan the play?

Precaution play

24 Game all; dealer South. Contract: 6C by South.

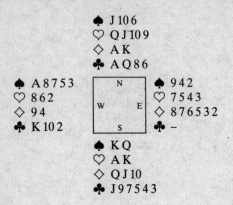

```
              ♠ J 10 6
              ♡ Q J 10 9
              ◇ A K
              ♣ A Q 8 6
  ♠ A 8 7 5 3        N        ♠ 9 4 2
  ♡ 8 6 2                     ♡ 7 5 4 3
  ◇ 9 4         W       E     ◇ 8 7 6 5 3 2
  ♣ K 10 2          S         ♣ -
              ♠ K Q
              ♡ A K
              ◇ Q J 10
              ♣ J 9 7 5 4 3
```

The play
South should lead the ♣J at trick three. Since the odds greatly
favour finessing West for the king of clubs it cannot cost to play
the knave first. If West has the singleton king, or East has all the
missing trumps, the knave will do no harm. If, however, West
has all three clubs playing the knave first will enable declarer to
pick up the suit without loss.

The principle
When a particular play cannot possibly cost a trick, and may
gain, it becomes rather more than a mere safety play. It is a
must. If declarer plays a low club to the queen, West will play
low and even though the queen wins nothing can prevent West
from making a trump trick.

25 Game all; dealer West. Contract: 4S by South.

♠ J9876
♡ 4
♢ K1053
♣ KJ4

♠ AKQ52
♡ A876
♢ 92
♣ 86

The bidding

S	W	N	E
—	1♡	Pass	2♡
2♠	Pass	4♠	Pass
Pass	Pass		

West leads the king of hearts. How should South plan the play?

Discovery play

25 Game all; dealer West. Contract: 4S by South.

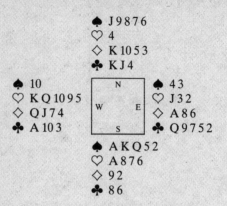

```
                    ♠ J 9 8 7 6
                    ♡ 4
                    ♢ K 10 5 3
                    ♣ K J 4
   ♠ 10                            ♠ 4 3
   ♡ K Q 10 9 5                    ♡ J 3 2
   ♢ Q J 7 4                       ♢ A 8 6
   ♣ A 10 3                        ♣ Q 9 7 5 2
                    ♠ A K Q 5 2
                    ♡ A 8 7 6
                    ♢ 9 2
                    ♣ 8 6
```

The play

Declarer should win the opening lead with the ♡A and draw
trumps, finishing in his own hand. He continues with a diamond,
losing dummy's king to East's ace. Later South has to take the
correct view in clubs: this he does by playing low towards dummy
and putting on the king after West has contributed the three. In
all, South loses two diamonds and one club.

The principle

South could lose four tricks if he misguesses the clubs and East
has the ♢A. There are scarcely enough high cards missing for
East to have *both* minor aces, thus it is important to discover if
East has the ♢A so that declarer may make the correct decision
in the other suit. Many 'guesses' can be averted by this type of
play.

26 E-W game; dealer North. Contract: 4S by South.

♠ A K 9 8
♡ J 7 6 4 2
♢ A 4 3
♣ 4

♠ Q J 7 6
♡ 9
♢ K 8 7
♣ A 9 7 6 5

The bidding

N	S
1♡	1♠
2♣	4♠

West leads the ace of hearts followed by the three of hearts. South ruffs the second round of hearts with the six of spades. How should he continue?

Cross-ruff

26 E-W game; dealer North. Contract: 4S by South.

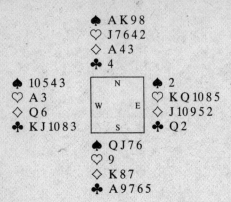

```
            ♠ A K 9 8
            ♡ J 7 6 4 2
            ♢ A 4 3
            ♣ 4
  ♠ 10 5 4 3              ♠ 2
  ♡ A 3        N          ♡ K Q 10 8 5
  ♢ Q 6     W   E         ♢ J 10 9 5 2
  ♣ K J 10 8 3   S        ♣ Q 2
            ♠ Q J 7 6
            ♡ 9
            ♢ K 8 7
            ♣ A 9 7 6 5
```

The play

With only three sure winners outside the trump suit (♢AK &
♣A) it is clear that declarer needs seven tricks from spades. This
means that he must proceed on cross-ruff lines, making his
trumps separately. He should cash the ♢AK and ♣A and ruff a
club with the ♠8. A heart is now ruffed with the ♠J, a club with
a ♠K, another heart with the ♠Q and a club with the ♠A.
Finally, declarer ruffs dummy's last heart with the ♠7. West is
welcome to overruff for declarer will then claim dummy's ♠9 for
his tenth trick.

The principle

It is *always* important to count your tricks. When setting out on a
cross-ruff it is *imperative*. Start by counting the winners in the
side suits. Subtract from the total you require. The remainder is
the number of trump tricks you must make. In this example you
will notice that provided declarer scores two low ruffs he is
home. The four honours yield four tricks and the two remaining
spades combine to make the vital tenth trick. A further point of
technique is illustrated by South's action in cashing his side-suit
winners first. If he fails to do this you will observe that West can
discard a diamond and South will then be unable to enjoy both
his diamond winners.

27 Love all; dealer East. Contract: 5C by South.

♠ A K Q 4
♡ 6 4 2
♢ A Q 3
♣ J 7 4

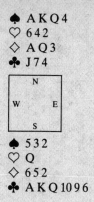

♠ 5 3 2
♡ Q
♢ 6 5 2
♣ A K Q 10 9 6

The bidding

S	W	N	E
—	—	—	1♡
2♣	Pass	2♡	Pass
3♣	Pass	5♣	Pass
Pass	Pass		

West leads the knave of hearts. East wins the king and plays the ace of hearts. How should South plan the play?

Throw-in

27 Love all; dealer East. Contract: 5C by South.

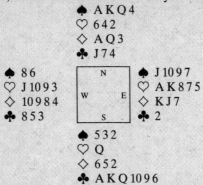

```
             ♠ A K Q 4
             ♡ 6 4 2
             ◇ A Q 3
             ♣ J 7 4
♠ 8 6              N          ♠ J 10 9 7
♡ J 10 9 3                    ♡ A K 8 7 5
◇ 10 9 8 4   W       E        ◇ K J 7
♣ 8 5 3            S          ♣ 2
             ♠ 5 3 2
             ♡ Q
             ◇ 6 5 2
             ♣ A K Q 10 9 6
```

The play

If the spades break 3-3 or the ◇K is right, declarer is home. However, both are against the odds, especially the latter, since East must surely hold the ◇K to justify his opening bid. Declarer should ruff the second heart and play four rounds of trumps, throwing a diamond from dummy. Now two rounds of spades and a heart ruff will leave the following position:

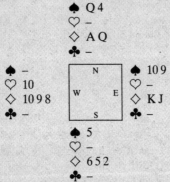

```
             ♠ Q 4
             ♡ –
             ◇ A Q
             ♣ –
♠ –                N          ♠ 10 9
♡ 10                          ♡ –
◇ 10 9 8     W       E        ◇ K J
♣ –                S          ♣ –
             ♠ 5
             ♡ –
             ◇ 6 5 2
             ♣ –
```

The ♠Q followed by the ♠4 will force East to concede the last two diamond tricks to dummy.

The principle
When a vital card – in this case the ◇K – appears certain to be
wrong declarer should look for an alternative line to the simple
finesse. The throw-in, forcing a defender to lead into your tenace, is often a viable ploy. Frequently it will extract the extra
trick from a powerless defence.

*

28 Love all; dealer South. Contract: 4S by South.

♠ A 10 9 3
♡ 10 8 3
◇ Q 10 8
♣ K 10 6

♠ K Q 8 7 5
♡ 6 4
◇ K J 9
♣ A J 3

The bidding

S	W	N	E
1♠	3♡	3♠	Pass
4♠	Pass	Pass	Pass

West starts with three top hearts, East petering with the five and
two and then discarding the two of clubs. South ruffs and plays
the king of spades, East discarding the two of diamonds. A low
spade to dummy's nine (East throwing the five of clubs) and a
diamond to the king and ace gives West the lead once more.
West exits with the six of diamonds. How should declarer plan
the play?

Counting and safety play

28 Love all; dealer South. Contract: 4S by South.

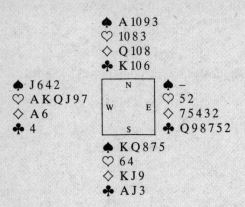

```
              ♠ A 10 9 3
              ♡ 10 8 3
              ◇ Q 10 8
              ♣ K 10 6
♠ J 6 4 2                      ♠ –
♡ A K Q J 9 7    N            ♡ 5 2
◇ A 6         W     E         ◇ 7 5 4 3 2
♣ 4              S            ♣ Q 9 8 7 5 2
              ♠ K Q 8 7 5
              ♡ 6 4
              ◇ K J 9
              ♣ A J 3
```

The play
South should win the second diamond and draw trumps. He
should continue with a low club to the king and confidently
finesse East for the queen. Since West has shown six hearts, four
spades and two diamonds, he cannot hold more than one club.
Thus the finesse is a certainty.

The principle
When considering a finesse there is no better guide than the
count of the hand. Often it is necessary to rely on inference,
rather than hard facts, but when the count is complete a doubtful
finesse can be turned into a certain winning play. Note also
South's safety play in the trump suit: the king first, to guard
against either defender holding four to the knave.

29 E-W game; dealer North. Contract: 4H by South.

♠ J 5
♡ K Q 4 2
◇ A Q J 9 4
♣ 8 5

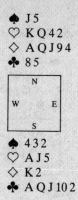

♠ 4 3 2
♡ A J 5
◇ K 2
♣ A Q J 10 2

The bidding

N	S
1◇	2♣
2◇	2♡*
3♡	3♠§
4♡	

(*A difficult rebid. South hopes partner will be able to bid no trumps)

(§The fourth suit – forcing – looking for a spade stop for 3NT)

Despite these awkward manoeuvres in the bidding N-S arrive in the best contract. West leads the seven of spades. East wins the first two spade tricks with the ace and queen and continues with the nine of spades. How should declarer plan the play?

Trump control

29 E-W game: dealer North. Contract: 4H by South.

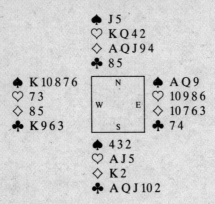

```
                    ♠ J 5
                    ♡ K Q 4 2
                    ◇ A Q J 9 4
                    ♣ 8 5
    ♠ K 10 8 7 6         N         ♠ A Q 9
    ♡ 7 3                          ♡ 10 9 8 6
    ◇ 8 5           W       E      ◇ 10 7 6 3
    ♣ K 9 6 3           S          ♣ 7 4
                    ♠ 4 3 2
                    ♡ A J 5
                    ◇ K 2
                    ♣ A Q J 10 2
```

The play
South should discard a club from dummy. He wins the next trick, draws trumps and claims the rest. If he fails to play this way the 4-2 trump break will defeat him.

The principle
A 4-3 trump holding needs special care since the outstanding break is likely to be 4-2 (48%) rather than 3-3 (36%). Whenever possible refuse the force if you would have to rely on a 3-3 trump division.

30 Game all; dealer West. Contract: 6S by South.

♠ A J 7 3
♡ A 3 2
◇ 8 6 3 2
♣ K 5

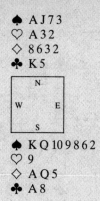

♠ K Q 10 9 8 6 2
♡ 9
◇ A Q 5
♣ A 8

The bidding

S	W	N	E
—	3♡	Pass	Pass
4♠	Pass	5♡	Pass
6♠	Pass	Pass	Pass

West leads the king of hearts. How should South plan the play?

Elimination with loser on loser

30 Game all; dealer West. Contract: 6S by South.

```
              ♠ A J 7 3
              ♡ A 3 2
              ♢ 8 6 3 2
              ♣ K 5
♠ -                          ♠ 5 4
♡ K Q J 10 8 7 5             ♡ 6 4
♢ K J 9                      ♢ 10 7 4
♣ 10 9 7                     ♣ Q J 6 4 3 2
              ♠ K Q 10 9 8 6 2
              ♡ 9
              ♢ A Q 5
              ♣ A 8
```

The play
There are eleven tricks on top and the extra one must come from diamonds or a ruff and discard. Declarer should win the opening lead with the ♡A, draw trumps and ruff a heart. The ♣A is cashed followed by the ♣K which gives dummy the lead once more. The ♡3 comes next and when East fails to follow South should discard his ♢5. Whatever West plays will ensure that declarer makes the remainder of the tricks.

The principle
Rather than bank everything on a successful finesse, declarer should search for an extra chance to improve on an even money proposition. In the above example the small diamond is an inevitable loser. However, declarer exchanges it for a losing heart with the effect that West is placed on lead. As both suits (hearts and clubs) have been eliminated, West is forced to provide South with his twelfth trick.

31 Game all; dealer South. Contract: 4H by South.

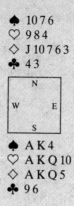

♠ 10 7 6
♡ 9 8 4
♢ J 10 7 6 3
♣ 4 3

♠ A K 4
♡ A K Q 10
♢ A K Q 5
♣ 9 6

The bidding

S	N
2♣	2♢
2♡	3♢
4♢	4♡
Pass	

West leads the king of clubs and continues with a club to East's ace. East switches to the five of spades. How should declarer plan the play?

Trump control

31. Game all; dealer South.   Contract: 4H by South.

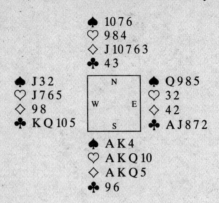

```
              ♠ 10 7 6
              ♡ 9 8 4
              ◇ J 10 7 6 3
              ♣ 4 3
  ♠ J 3 2                    ♠ Q 9 8 5
  ♡ J 7 6 5       N          ♡ 3 2
  ◇ 9 8       W       E      ◇ 4 2
  ♣ K Q 10 5                 ♣ A J 8 7 2
                   S
              ♠ A K 4
              ♡ A K Q 10
              ◇ A K Q 5
              ♣ 9 6
```

The play
South should win the ♠A and play the ♡A followed by the
♡10! He can count 3 hearts, 2 spades and 5 diamonds. The
danger is that if either defender holds ♡Jxxx he will defer ruffing
diamonds until the fourth round, thus South will lose 2 clubs, 1
heart and 1 spade. If the defence win the knave of hearts at trick
five, dummy can control the force should they persevere with
clubs.

The principle
Once you appreciate that you can afford to lose a trump trick,
ensure that you lose it at a time to suit your convenience – not
when it is fatal.

32. Game all; dealer South.   Contract: 6D by South.

♠ 8 6
♡ A K 6
♢ K 9 2
♣ A Q J 5 2

♠ A K 5
♡ J 4 2
♢ A J 8 5 4
♣ K 8

The bidding

S	N
1♢	3♣
3♢	4♢
4♠	5♡
5NT	6♢
Pass	

Having agreed on diamonds and cue bid the major suit aces, South employs the grand slam force (5NT) to see if his partner holds both the king and queen of diamonds. With the queen of diamonds missing the small slam is enough. West leads the queen of spades, East following with the three. How should South plan the play?

Safety play

32. Game all; dealer South.   Contract: 6D by South.

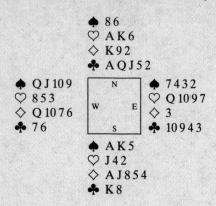

```
                    ♠ 86
                    ♡ A K 6
                    ◇ K 9 2
                    ♣ A Q J 5 2
  ♠ Q J 10 9       ┌─────────┐       ♠ 7 4 3 2
  ♡ 8 5 3          │    N    │       ♡ Q 10 9 7
  ◇ Q 10 7 6       │ W     E │       ◇ 3
  ♣ 7 6            │    S    │       ♣ 10 9 4 3
                   └─────────┘
                    ♠ A K 5
                    ♡ J 4 2
                    ◇ A J 8 5 4
                    ♣ K 8
```

The play

South should win the spade lead and play the ◇A followed by a small diamond to dummy's nine (assuming West plays low). Twelve tricks are now assured. Should West follow with a diamond honour on the second round South has no further problems.

The principle

K9x opposite AJxxx is an example of the many combinations which afford a safety play to restrict the losers to one. Here are some others:

(1) AK9xx   (2) AJxx
     Jxx   K9xx

You will note the similarity. In each case you are missing five cards including the queen and the ten.

(1) Play the ace and, unless the ten appears, lead low to the knave.

(2) Play the ace and lead small to the nine.

33. Love all; dealer South.   Contract: 4H by South.

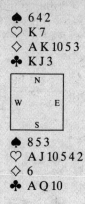

                ♠ 6 4 2
                ♡ K 7
                ◇ A K 10 5 3
                ♣ K J 3

                ♠ 8 5 3
                ♡ A J 10 5 4 2
                ◇ 6
                ♣ A Q 10

The bidding

S	W	N	E
1♡	1♠	2◇	Pass
2♡	Pass	4♡	Pass
Pass	Pass		

West leads three top spades, East discarding the two of clubs on the third round, and switches to the nine of clubs. South wins with the ace, plays a heart to the king and then returns the seven of hearts to his ten, West throwing a spade. How should South continue?

Trump reduction
(Trump coup)

33. Love all; dealer South.   Contract: 4H by South.

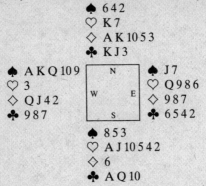

```
               ♠ 6 4 2
               ♡ K 7
               ◇ A K 10 5 3
               ♣ K J 3
♠ A K Q 10 9   ┌─────────┐   ♠ J 7
♡ 3            │   N     │   ♡ Q 9 8 6
◇ Q J 4 2      │ W     E │   ◇ 9 8 7
♣ 9 8 7        │   S     │   ♣ 6 5 4 2
               └─────────┘
               ♠ 8 5 3
               ♡ A J 10 5 4 2
               ◇ 6
               ♣ A Q 10
```

The play
South should play a diamond to the ace and ruff a diamond. Continue with the ♣10 to the knave and ruff a second diamond. When dummy is re-entered with the ♣K the stage is set to pick up East's ♡Q. This will be the position with North to play:

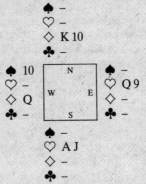

```
           ♠ –
           ♡ –
           ◇ K 10
           ♣ –
♠ 10       ┌─────────┐   ♠ –
♡ –        │   N     │   ♡ Q 9
◇ Q        │ W     E │   ◇ –
♣ –        │   S     │   ♣ –
           └─────────┘
           ♠ –
           ♡ A J
           ◇ –
           ♣ –
```

The principle
When the absence of trumps in dummy precludes the capture of an opponent's trump honour by a direct finesse, declarer may still succeed by shortening his trumps to the same number as his opponent. Then the play of *any* card through that defender will pick up his trump honour.

34. Love all; dealer South.   Contract: 4S by South.

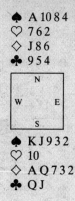

♠ A 10 8 4
♡ 7 6 2
♢ J 8 6
♣ 9 5 4

♠ K J 9 3 2
♡ 10
♢ A Q 7 3 2
♣ Q J

The bidding

S	W	N	E
1♠	2♡	2♠	4♡
4♠	Pass	Pass	Pass

West leads the two of clubs to East's ace. East returns the three of hearts and West wins with the knave. West cashes the king of clubs and continues with the ace of hearts which South ruffs. How should declarer plan the play?

Hopeful assumption

34. Love all; dealer South.   Contract: 4S by South.

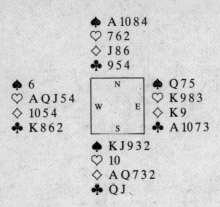

♠ A 10 8 4
♡ 7 6 2
♢ J 8 6
♣ 9 5 4

♠ 6
♡ A Q J 5 4
♢ 10 5 4
♣ K 8 6 2

♠ Q 7 5
♡ K 9 8 3
♢ K 9
♣ A 10 7 3

♠ K J 9 3 2
♡ 10
♢ A Q 7 3 2
♣ Q J

The play
Declarer should play a spade to dummy's ace and return the
♠10, allowing it to ride when East plays low. The diamond
finesse comes next followed by the ♣K. Declarer cashes the ♢A
and continues with a diamond to dummy's knave. He can now
claim the remainder of the tricks.

The principle
At first blush it appears that South enjoyed more than his share
of good luck. However, the point is that *he must find East with*
♢:Kx. Accordingly, he plays on this optimistic assumption. The
play to the first four tricks suggests that West has five hearts and
four clubs. So if East is assumed to have ♢Kx, West has three
diamonds *and therefore a singleton spade.* Declarer's play of the
spade suit is not inspiration – merely a logical extension of his
'hopeful assumption'. This type of play is the converse of a safety
play. When prospects are poor and only one distribution permits
you to succeed – assume that distribution exists and form your
plan accordingly.

35. N-S game; dealer South. Contract: 3NT by South.

♠ Q 10 3
♡ A K J 9
♢ 10 8 2
♣ 10 6 4

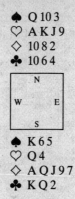

♠ K 6 5
♡ Q 4
♢ A Q J 9 7
♣ K Q 2

The bidding

S	W	N	E
1♢	Pass	1♡	1♠
2NT	Pass	3NT	Pass
Pass	Pass		

West leads the eight of spades. How should South plan the play?

Blocking play

35. N-S game; dealer South. Contract: 3NT by South.

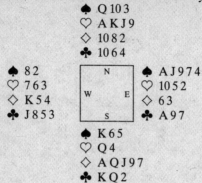

```
                  ♠ Q 10 3
                  ♡ A K J 9
                  ♢ 10 8 2
                  ♣ 10 6 4
    ♠ 8 2             N           ♠ A J 9 7 4
    ♡ 7 6 3                       ♡ 10 5 2
    ♢ K 5 4        W     E        ♢ 6 3
    ♣ J 8 5 3         S           ♣ A 9 7
                  ♠ K 6 5
                  ♡ Q 4
                  ♢ A Q J 9 7
                  ♣ K Q 2
```

The play

South should put in dummy's ♠Q, making it impossible for East
to find a successful counter. If East wins, he will not be able to
continue spades without conceding an extra trick. If he ducks,
South will be able to make two spade tricks. Declarer should
continue by taking the diamond finesse to make certain of at
least nine tricks. Note what happens should South fail to contribute the ♠Q at trick one. If instead he plays the ♠10, East
will cover with the ♠J and now nothing can prevent the defence
from coming to five tricks.

The principle

When a defender leads a short suit, through your combined
honour cards (in dummy and declarer's hand), the smooth run of
the suit can often be disrupted by the second player contributing
a high honour. The defender with the length must then either
concede a trick or a tempo. This is a similar situation to the
above:

```
                   K 9 3
         10 4               A J 8 7 6
                   Q 5 2
```

When the ten is led North plays the king, and East is faced with
the same dilemma.

36. E-W game; dealer South.   Contract: 4S by South.

♠ 8 4 2
♡ 9
◇ A Q 8 7
♣ A K 7 4 2

♠ A Q 6 5 3
♡ J 8
◇ K J 5 3
♣ Q 3

The bidding

S	N
1♠	2♣
2◇	2♡*
2♠	4♠

(*The fourth suit – forcing—asking for more information)

West leads the king of hearts and then switches to the knave of clubs. How should South plan the play?

Safety play

36. E-W game; dealer South.   Contract: 4S by South.

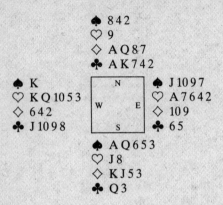

```
                  ♠ 842
                  ♡ 9
                  ◇ AQ87
                  ♣ AK742
   ♠ K                         ♠ J1097
   ♡ KQ1053            N       ♡ A7642
   ◇ 642           W       E   ◇ 109
   ♣ J1098             S       ♣ 65
                  ♠ AQ653
                  ♡ J8
                  ◇ KJ53
                  ♣ Q3
```

The play

South should win the club in hand and cash the ♠A. When the
king falls he cannot lose more than two spades and one heart.

The principle

Taking the spade suit in isolation declarer must lose at least one
trick. In the above example his paramount concern is to restrict
his losses to two. In such circumstances it is correct to cash the
ace in case there is a blank king. If East has the ♠K nothing is
lost since declarer will subsequently play a spade towards his
queen. Had West followed to the first round of spades with any
card but the king, declarer could have ruffed his heart loser in
dummy and played the last spade, covering whatever East
played.

37. Game all; dealer South.   Contract: 6S by South.

♠ K J 7 5
♥ A J 10 9 5
♦ 6
♣ Q 4 2

♠ A Q 10 9 8 6 3
♥ Q 4
♦ K Q J
♣ A

The bidding

S	N
2♠	3♠
4♣	4♥
4NT	5♦
6♠	

West leads the knave of clubs. How should South plan the play?

The decoy coup

37. Game all; dealer South.   Contract: 6S by South.

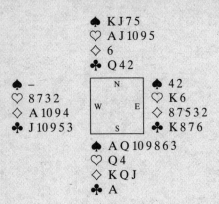

```
                  ♠ K J 7 5
                  ♡ A J 10 9 5
                  ◇ 6
                  ♣ Q 4 2
     ♠ —                          ♠ 4 2
     ♡ 8 7 3 2          N         ♡ K 6
     ◇ A 10 9 4      W     E      ◇ 8 7 5 3 2
     ♣ J 10 9 5 3       S         ♣ K 8 7 6
                  ♠ A Q 10 9 8 6 3
                  ♡ Q 4
                  ◇ K Q J
                  ♣ A
```

The play
South should cover the knave of clubs with dummy's queen. No doubt East will follow with the king and South, perforce, wins the ace. The heart finesse should be taken at trick two in order to avoid the possibility of West's signalling with a high diamond. If East falls into the trap of believing that South has a second club, declarer is home.

The principle
When a high card is of no value to declarer it can sometimes be used as a decoy to deflect the opposition from the best defence. Here the ♣Q is irrelevant to South. Success will depend on the position of the ♡K, but it costs nothing to give East an opportunity to go wrong. With ♣Ax South would almost certainly try dummy's queen at trick one, so, odd as it seems, East's problem is a very real one.

38. E-W game; dealer West.   Contract: 4H by South.

♠ A 2
♡ A 10 5
♢ 9 7 5 4 2
♣ Q 6 4

♠ 9 6
♡ K J 9 8 7 2
♢ A K J
♣ 5 3

The bidding

S	W	N	E
—	1♠	Pass	2♠
3♡	Pass	4♡	Pass
Pass	Pass		

West leads the four of spades. How should South plan the play?

38. E-W game; dealer West.   Contract: 4H by South.

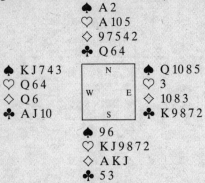

♠ A 2
♡ A 10 5
◇ 9 7 5 4 2
♣ Q 6 4

♠ K J 7 4 3
♡ Q 6 4
◇ Q 6
♣ A J 10

♠ Q 10 8 5
♡ 3
◇ 10 8 3
♣ K 9 8 7 2

♠ 9 6
♡ K J 9 8 7 2
◇ A K J
♣ 5 3

The play

The fact that West has chosen to lead from a broken suit (with the king and queen of spades he would surely have led a top honour) affords the assumption that he is unlikely to hold *both* the ace and king of clubs, or both the king and queen of spades, for with those cards a club or spade lead might appear more attractive. Thus if East is to be given one top card in each black suit, West must be credited with the red suit queens to justify his opening bid. Once South has placed all the key cards – albeit inferentially – the basic plan is simple. Play West for the red suit queens, finessing the case of the ♡Q and playing for the drop in the case of the ◇Q. However, it costs nothing to lead a club towards dummy early on and this little diversion may help to confirm the original diagnosis. So, South wins the ♠A, then plays a heart to the king and a low club towards dummy. West will no doubt go in with the ten, retaining a tenace position in case South has the king, and East will win the trick. Case established! The defence cash a spade and a second club, but declarer takes the next trick, pulls trumps via the finesse and then lays down the ◇AK.

The principle

Why an opponent does not lead a certain card can be almost as significant as the actual card he selects. Combine the clues derived from the opening lead and the information gained in the bidding and you will sometimes get a complete picture of the hand at trick one. In the above case declarer could infer the position of every relevant card as soon as West made his opening lead.

*

39. Love all; dealer South.   Contract: 3NT by South.

```
              ♠ 6 4
              ♡ K
              ♢ A K 7 5 2
              ♣ Q 10 9 7 4
```

```
              ♠ A K Q 5 3
              ♡ A 5 2
              ♢ 9 8 3
              ♣ 5 3
```

The bidding

S	N
1♠	2♢
2♠	3♣
3NT	

West leads the queen of hearts. On the ace of diamonds East follows with the knave. How should declarer plan the play?

Unblocking play

39. Love all; dealer South.   Contract: 3NT by South.

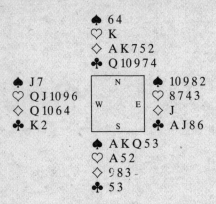

```
              ♠ 64
              ♡ K
              ◇ A K 7 5 2
              ♣ Q 10 9 7 4
  ♠ J 7            N        ♠ 10 9 8 2
  ♡ Q J 10 9 6              ♡ 8 7 4 3
  ◇ Q 10 6 4   W      E     ◇ J
  ♣ K 2            S        ♣ A J 8 6
              ♠ A K Q 5 3
              ♡ A 5 2
              ◇ 9 8 3
              ♣ 5 3
```

The play

South should unblock with the ◇8 and then play a low diamond
to the nine. If West accepts this trick, declarer will subsequently
be able to finesse against West's ◇Q, making 4 diamonds, 3
spades and 2 hearts. If West refuses the diamond, declarer
should play a low spade from both hands. He will now make 4
spades, 3 diamonds and 2 hearts.

The principle

If one trick has to be lost it is important to handle the suit
concerned in such a way that an adverse distribution can be
overcome. When East follows with the knave (or any honour
card) it is important to get rid of the nine or eight so as to create
a finessing position against West. Note that where West refuses
the second diamond it is essential to play a low spade from both
hands. This preserves the communications where the spades are
4-2.

40. E-W game; dealer South.   Contract: 6S by South.

♠ K 6
♡ 10
◇ A Q J 10 9
♣ A Q J 10 2

♠ A Q 10 9 8 7 5
♡ 9 7
◇ K
♣ K 6 4

The bidding

S	N
4♠	4NT
5◇	6♠

West leads the ace of hearts, East contributing the queen. West continues with a second heart, dummy's six of spades winning the trick. How should South plan the play?

Trump reduction
(Grand coup)

40. E-W game; dealer South. Contract: 6S by South.

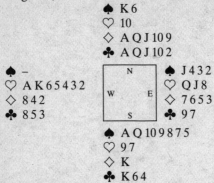

♠ K 6
♥ 10
♦ A Q J 10 9
♣ A Q J 10 2

♠ –
♥ A K 6 5 4 3 2
♦ 8 4 2
♣ 8 5 3

♠ J 4 3 2
♥ Q J 8
♦ 7 6 5 3
♣ 9 7

♠ A Q 10 9 8 7 5
♥ 9 7
♦ K
♣ K 6 4

The play

The only danger is a bad trump break and West's defence bodes ill. South should play the ♦A and *ruff* a diamond. Return to dummy with the ♠K to learn the bad news. However, a second diamond ruff is followed by a club to the ten and a third diamond ruff. Now a club to dummy leaves the following position:

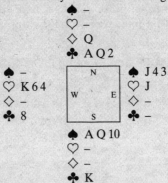

♠ –
♥ –
♦ Q
♣ A Q 2

♠ –
♥ K 6 4
♦ –
♣ 8

♠ J 4 3
♥ J
♦ –
♣ –

♠ A Q 10
♥ –
♦ –
♣ K

The ♦Q is played from dummy. East can procrastinate by discarding the ♥J, in which case South throws the ♣K, but the next lead leaves East helpless.

The principle
Sometimes it may be impossible to counteract a bad trump break by natural means. With no trump in dummy to play through East's holding you must reduce your own trumps to the same number as your opponent. A Grand Coup arises when you have to ruff *winners* in order to effect that reduction.

*

41. Game all; dealer West.   Contract: 6H by South.

♠ –
♡ Q 9 7 5 3
♢ K 6 4
♣ 9 7 6 4 3

♠ A 4 3
♡ A K J 10 8 6
♢ Q 3
♣ A Q

The bidding

S	W	N	E
—	1♠	Pass	Pass
Double	2♣	Pass	Pass
4♡	Pass	4♠	Pass
5♣	Pass	5♢	Pass
6♡	Pass	Pass	Pass

West leads the king of spades. How should declarer plan the play?

Morton's Fork coup

41. Game all; dealer West.   Contract: 6H by South.

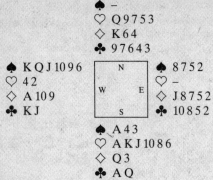

```
              ♠ —
              ♡ Q 9 7 5 3
              ◇ K 6 4
              ♣ 9 7 6 4 3
♠ K Q J 10 9 6    N     ♠ 8 7 5 2
♡ 4 2                   ♡ —
◇ A 10 9      W     E   ◇ J 8 7 5 2
♣ K J            S      ♣ 10 8 5 2
              ♠ A 4 3
              ♡ A K J 10 8 6
              ◇ Q 3
              ♣ A Q
```

The play

South must ruff the spade lead in dummy, enter hand with a
trump and play a diamond towards the king. Assuming the ◇K
wins, a second trump is won by South, the ♠A is cashed, dummy
throwing a diamond, and a spade is ruffed in dummy. South
follows with a diamond to the queen and West is end-played.
Note, if West goes up with the ◇A on the first round declarer
has a parking place for his ♣Q.

The principle

This coup presents a defender with the choice of either taking a
trick by playing his ace on thin air, or ducking and laying himself
open to an end-play. Alternatively, if the trick is not accepted at
once, a subsequent discard may deprive the defence of their trick
in that suit altogether. A slight alteration to the N-S cards gives
an illustration of this last variety. 6H by West. Lead ♠K.

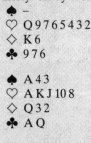

```
              ♠ —
              ♡ Q 9 7 6 5 4 3 2
              ◇ K 6
              ♣ 9 7 6

              ♠ A 4 3
              ♡ A K J 10 8
              ◇ Q 3 2
              ♣ A Q
```

The coup derives its name from Cardinal Morton who was a zealous collector of taxes for Henry VII. He worked on the principle that if a man lived ostentatiously he could afford to pay, while if he lived frugally he must have plenty stacked away. In either case he was impaled on Morton's Fork.

*

42. N-S game; dealer North. Contract: 3NT by South.

♠ 10 2
♡ 3 2
♢ A K Q J 4
♣ K J 10 6

♠ A J 9 6
♡ K J 7
♢ 7 3 2
♣ Q 8 4

The bidding

S	W	N	E
—	—	1♢	1♡
1♠	2♡	Pass	Pass
2NT	Pass	3NT	Pass
Pass	Pass		

West leads the four of hearts. East wins with the ace and returns the ten of hearts. How should declarer plan the play?

Blocking play

42. N-S game; dealer North. Contract: 3NT by South.

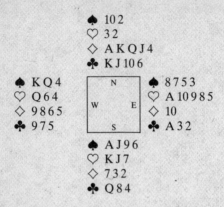

```
                ♠ 10 2
                ♡ 3 2
                ◇ A K Q J 4
                ♣ K J 10 6
♠ K Q 4          ┌──────────┐        ♠ 8 7 5 3
♡ Q 6 4          │    N     │        ♡ A 10 9 8 5
◇ 9 8 6 5        │ W     E  │        ◇ 10
♣ 9 7 5          │    S     │        ♣ A 3 2
                 └──────────┘
                ♠ A J 9 6
                ♡ K J 7
                ◇ 7 3 2
                ♣ Q 8 4
```

The play
South should insert the ♡K at trick two in an effort to block the
suit. It seems likely from the bidding and the play to the first two
tricks that West started with ♡Qxx. If South makes the mistake of
trying the ♡J West will clear the suit and eventually East must get
in with the ♣A to take five tricks. Having won with the ♡K South
should establish the club suit before turning his attention to
diamonds.

The principle
Opportunities to block the easy flow of a suit are quite common.
the bidding and play in this case indicate that West probably
started with ♡Qxx; thus declarer's best chance is to disrupt the
communications. Maybe East's play of the ♡10 was a little naive,
but whatever heart he returns South should play the same way.

43. E-W game; dealer South.   Contract: 4H by South.

♠ 5 4 3 2
♡ A J 5
♢ 5 4 2
♣ K 3 2

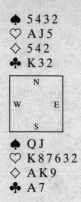

♠ Q J
♡ K 8 7 6 3 2
♢ A K 9
♣ A 7

The bidding

S	W	N	E
1♡	1♠	2♡	Pass
4♡	Pass	Pass	Pass

West plays the ace, king and ten of spades, East following to the first round and then discarding the six of diamonds and four of clubs. South ruffs and plays the king of hearts followed by a heart to the ace, West discarding a spade on the second heart. How should South continue?

Double squeeze

43. E-W game; dealer South.   Contract: 4H by South.

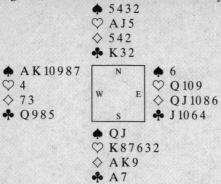

♠ 5 4 3 2
♡ A J 5
◇ 5 4 2
♣ K 3 2

♠ A K 10 9 8 7
♡ 4
◇ 7 3
♣ Q 9 8 5

♠ 6
♡ Q 10 9
◇ Q J 10 8 6
♣ J 10 6 4

♠ Q J
♡ K 8 7 6 3 2
◇ A K 9
♣ A 7

The play

South should give East his trump trick to prepare the ground for a squeeze. West is known to hold the spades, and if East alone holds the diamonds the squeeze will be automatic. No doubt East will switch to a diamond. South wins, cashes his second diamond and then runs off the trumps. This will be the position before the last trump is played.

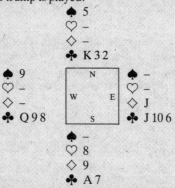

♠ 5
♡ –
◇ –
♣ K 3 2

♠ 9
♡ –
◇ –
♣ Q 9 8

♠ –
♡ –
◇ J
♣ J 10 6

♠ –
♡ 8
◇ 9
♣ A 7

On the ♡8 West is forced to throw a club, dummy discards the ♠5, and East must also throw a club otherwise declarer's ◇9 becomes good. The ♣A, ♣K and *master* ♣3 take the last three tricks.

94

The principle

A double squeeze involves three suits. If one opponent guards one suit exclusively while his partner controls another, then neither can guard the third. In the above example West guards spades while East guards diamonds so neither can retain control over clubs. Note, it is essential that the menace cards lie *over* the cards that guard them. Exchange the ♠5 and ◇9 and the squeeze doesn't work.

*

44. Game all; dealer South.   Contract: 3NT by South.

♠ A Q J 8 7
♡ K 7
◇ 7 3 2
♣ J 8 6

♠ 3 2
♡ A 8 3 2
◇ A K 5 4
♣ A K 3

The bidding

S	N
1♡	1♠
2NT	3NT

West leads the queen of diamonds. How should South plan the play?

Ducking

44. Game all; dealer South. Contract: 3NT by South.

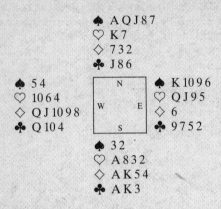

```
                    ♠ A Q J 8 7
                    ♡ K 7
                    ◇ 7 3 2
                    ♣ J 8 6
    ♠ 5 4              N          ♠ K 10 9 6
    ♡ 10 6 4                      ♡ Q J 9 5
    ◇ Q J 10 9 8   W       E      ◇ 6
    ♣ Q 10 4            S         ♣ 9 7 5 2
                    ♠ 3 2
                    ♡ A 8 3 2
                    ◇ A K 5 4
                    ♣ A K 3
```

The play
South has six top tricks outside the spade suit and therefore
requires precisely three spades for his contract. He wins the
diamond lead, but if he takes the spade finesse, and East holds
off, he will not make more than two spade tricks. The solution is
to duck first round of spades completely, permitting East to win
with the ♠9. Declarer wins the return in his hand and plays a
spade to the knave. East is welcome to this trick for declarer is
now certain to make three spade tricks – and his game.

The principle
When entries to one hand are restricted it is important for
declarer to manage the key suit in such a way that he obtains the
tricks he needs even against an adverse distribution. In this case
he needs exactly three tricks and has only one outside entry,
therefore to duck on the first round is correct. If he needs four or
five tricks, a small spade to the knave would be the obvious line.

45. E-W game; dealer South.   Contract: 3NT by South.

$\spadesuit$ J32
$\heartsuit$ A2
$\diamondsuit$ A85
$\clubsuit$ K10975

$\spadesuit$ AK6
$\heartsuit$ 10954
$\diamondsuit$ K106
$\clubsuit$ QJ8

The bidding

S	N
1NT	3NT

West leads the six of hearts. How should declarer plan the play?

Blocking play

45. E-W game; dealer South.   Contract: 3NT by South.

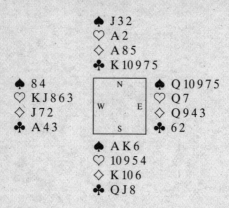

```
                    ♠ J 3 2
                    ♡ A 2
                    ♢ A 8 5
                    ♣ K 10 9 7 5
    ♠ 8 4              N          ♠ Q 10 9 7 5
    ♡ K J 8 6 3                   ♡ Q 7
    ♢ J 7 2         W     E       ♢ Q 9 4 3
    ♣ A 4 3            S          ♣ 6 2
                    ♠ A K 6
                    ♡ 10 9 5 4
                    ♢ K 10 6
                    ♣ Q J 8
```

The play

South should play dummy's ♡A. It is practically certain from
West's lead that he has not got the three top honours, therefore
declarer's best chance lies in blocking the suit. After the ♣A is
knocked out South sails home with 4 clubs, 2 spades, 2 diamonds
and 1 heart. Note what happens if South ducks the opening lead.
East wins and returns a heart. Now the defence will take four
hearts and the ace of clubs.

The principle

Sometimes success or failure will turn on declarer's ability to
interrupt the flow of the enemy's suit. While it is often right to
sever the communications by ducking, it can be equally potent to
offer the defence the choice between following low and blocking
the suit, or throwing an honour card and establishing an extra
guard. The vital clue is usually the card led, perhaps reinforced
by the auction.

46. E-W game; dealer North.   Contract: 4H by South.

♠ J
♡ A 7 3
◇ K 7 5
♣ A K J 7 3 2

♠ A 8 6
♡ K Q 9 8 5
◇ 10 2
♣ 10 5 4

The bidding

S	N
1♣	1♡
3♣	4♣
4♡	

West leads the four of spades to East's king. How should South plan the play?

Trump control

46. E-W game; dealer North.   Contract: 4H by South.

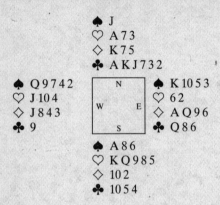

```
              ♠ J
              ♡ A 7 3
              ◇ K 7 5
              ♣ A K J 7 3 2

  ♠ Q 9 7 4 2      N        ♠ K 10 5 3
  ♡ J 10 4                  ♡ 6 2
  ◇ J 8 4 3    W       E    ◇ A Q 9 6
  ♣ 9              S        ♣ Q 8 6

              ♠ A 8 6
              ♡ K Q 9 8 5
              ◇ 10 2
              ♣ 10 5 4
```

The play
South should duck the ♠K! If East continues the suit declarer
ruffs in dummy, draws trumps and takes the club finesse. Once
South has refused to win the first trick the defence are powerless,
but note what happens if South wins the opening spade lead. He
can ruff *one* spade, cash the ♡A and return to hand and draw
trumps, but now, with the ♣Q guarded and offside, East can put
his partner in with a spade to make the lethal diamond switch.

The principle
This is an extension of the elementary concept of trump control.
Declarer withholds a side-suit ace so that dummy's trumps can
take care of a spade continuation and simultaneously monitor
the lines to communication between East and West.
'Don't play too quickly to the first trick' is excellent advice as this
example demonstrates.

47. E-W game; dealer South.   Contract: 4H doubled by South.

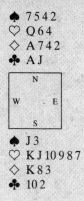

♠ 7 5 4 2
♡ Q 6 4
♢ A 7 4 2
♣ A J

♠ J 3
♡ K J 10 9 8 7
♢ K 8 3
♣ 10 2

The bidding

S	W	N	E
3♡	Double*	4♡	Double
Pass	Pass	Pass	
(*For take-out)			

West leads three top spades, East following suit. South ruffs and plays a heart to dummy's queen and East's ace. East switches to the queen of diamonds. How should declarer plan the play?

Triple squeeze

47. E-W game; dealer South.   Contract: 4H doubled by South.

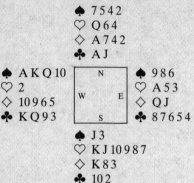

```
              ♠ 7 5 4 2
              ♡ Q 6 4
              ◇ A 7 4 2
              ♣ A J
  ♠ A K Q 10      N        ♠ 9 8 6
  ♡ 2                      ♡ A 5 3
  ◇ 10 9 6 5   W     E     ◇ Q J
  ♣ K Q 9 3      S         ♣ 8 7 6 5 4
              ♠ J 3
              ♡ K J 10 9 8 7
              ◇ K 8 3
              ♣ 10 2
```

The play

With precisely eight tricks on top declarer's only hope is a triple squeeze, the coup that produces *two* extra tricks. The diamond switch should be won in dummy and the trumps played out. This will be the position immediately before the last trump is cashed:

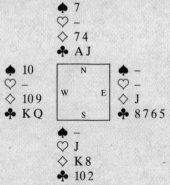

```
              ♠ 7
              ♡ —
              ◇ 7 4
              ♣ A J
  ♠ 10          N          ♠ —
  ♡ —                      ♡ —
  ◇ 10 9      W     E      ◇ J
  ♣ K Q         S          ♣ 8 7 6 5
              ♠ —
              ♡ J
              ◇ K 8
              ♣ 10 2
```

Declarer plays the ♡J and West has an impossible discard. Suppose he throws a diamond, dummy does likewise and now the ◇K8 squeezes West in the black suits. Should West throw the ♠10 on the ♡J, dummy is entered with the ♣A and now the ♠7 squeezes West once more. Note that the ◇K is the entry to declarer's hand, and that is why East's diamond switch was won in dummy.

The principle

The triple squeeze, or progressive squeeze as it is sometimes called, yields *two* extra tricks in the end-game. For this squeeze to be effective one player must guard three suits. When he has been squeezed out of one of his tricks pressure is continued with the established winner in what now becomes a simple squeeze.

*

48. Game all; dealer North.   Contract: 6S by South.

♠ 862
♡ A 10 7
◇ A J 4
♣ A K J 5

♠ A K 10 9 7 4
♡ Q
◇ K Q 3
♣ Q 8 2

The bidding

N	S
1♣	1♠
2NT	3♣
3♠	4NT
5♠	5NT
6◇	6♠

West leads the ten of diamonds. On the ace of spades East throws the nine of hearts. How should South plan the play?

103

Trump reduction
(Trump end-play)

48. Game all; dealer North.   Contract: 6S by South.

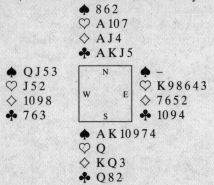

```
                    ♠ 8 6 2
                    ♡ A 10 7
                    ◇ A J 4
                    ♣ A K J 5
    ♠ Q J 5 3          N          ♠ —
    ♡ J 5 2                        ♡ K 9 8 6 4 3
    ◇ 10 9 8       W       E       ◇ 7 6 5 2
    ♣ 7 6 3                        ♣ 10 9 4
                        S
                    ♠ A K 10 9 7 4
                    ♡ Q
                    ◇ K Q 3
                    ♣ Q 8 2
```

The play

South must reduce his trumps to the same number as held by West. He cashes the ♡A and ruffs a heart, enters dummy with a diamond and ruffs a second heart. He now plans to strip West of his remaining plain cards. The exact distribution of the minors is not known but if he guesses correctly declarer will cash one more diamond and three clubs to arrive at this position.

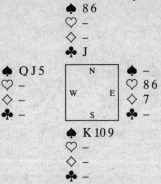

```
                    ♠ 8 6
                    ♡ —
                    ◇ —
                    ♣ J
    ♠ Q J 5            N          ♠ —
    ♡ —                            ♡ 8 6
    ◇ —            W       E       ◇ 7
    ♣ —                            ♣ —
                        S
                    ♠ K 10 9
                    ♡ —
                    ◇ —
                    ♣ —
```

A spade to the ten and knave end-plays West.

The principle
If unable to pick up an opponent's trumps that lie over you, you must reduce your own holding to the same number as his. You must also cash any winners that would otherwise provide him with a safe exit. Finally, throw him in so that he has to lead up to your trump tenace.

*

49. Game all; dealer South.   Contract: 6H by South.

<blockquote>
♠ J 9 4 3 2
♡ 7 4 3
◇ 9 5
♣ A 10 5
</blockquote>

<blockquote>
♠ A K 6
♡ A K Q J 10 9
◇ A K
♣ Q 8
</blockquote>

The bidding

S	N
2♣	2◇
3♡*	4♣
4◇	4♡
6♡	

(*Showing a solid suit)

West leads the four of clubs which is allowed to run to East's king. How should South plan the play?

Unblocking play

49. Game all; dealer South.   Contract: 6H by South.

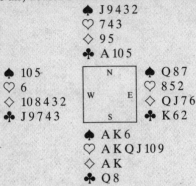

```
                    ♠ J 9 4 3 2
                    ♡ 7 4 3
                    ◇ 9 5
                    ♣ A 10 5
      ♠ 10 5                        ♠ Q 8 7
      ♡ 6                           ♡ 8 5 2
      ◇ 10 8 4 3 2                  ◇ Q J 7 6
      ♣ J 9 7 4 3                   ♣ K 6 2
                    ♠ A K 6
                    ♡ A K Q J 10 9
                    ◇ A K
                    ♣ Q 8
```

The play
South must jettison the ♣Q on East's king so that he has a
finessing position against the knave. Trumps are drawn and the
♠AK cashed in case the queen drops. When this chance fails
South plays a low club towards dummy, putting in the ten when
West plays low. The ♣A provides a discard for South's losing
spade. It is perhaps worth noting that West found the only lead
to embarrass declarer. Anything else would have made it easy to
establish the spade suit for discards.

The principle
By throwing a high card you prepare the ground for a finesse that
would not otherwise be available. This combination is similar to
the example above:

A 10 9 4

J 3

West leads a small card and East wins with the king. If entries to
the North hand are scarce it is correct to drop the knave.

50. Game all; dealer North.   Contract: 3NT by South.

♠ 5
♡ K Q 10 6
♢ A Q 5
♣ K Q 9 5 3

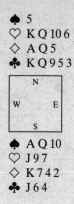

♠ A Q 10
♡ J 9 7
♢ K 7 4 2
♣ J 6 4

The bidding

N	S
1♣	1♢
1♡	2NT
3NT	

West leads the four of spades, East contributing the knave. How should declarer plan the play?

Timing

50. Game all; dealer North.   Contract: 3NT by South.

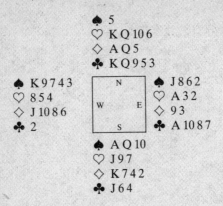

```
                    ♠ 5
                    ♡ K Q 10 6
                    ♢ A Q 5
                    ♣ K Q 9 5 3
    ♠ K 9 7 4 3          N          ♠ J 8 6 2
    ♡ 8 5 4                          ♡ A 3 2
    ♢ J 10 8 6      W       E        ♢ 9 3
    ♣ 2                  S          ♣ A 10 8 7
                    ♠ A Q 10
                    ♡ J 9 7
                    ♢ K 7 4 2
                    ♣ J 6 4
```

The play
South wins with the ♣Q, enters dummy with a diamond and
plays a low club *towards the knave*. If East goes up with the ace,
there are nine tricks. If he ducks, South's knave wins and the
♡A is knocked out – again guaranteeing nine tricks. Should
declarer make the mistake of playing a club towards dummy, or
playing hearts before clubs, the contract will fail. It is true that
South will often go unpunished for his poor timing – but not with
this distribution.

The principle
When tricks are required from any given suit it is necessary to
consider whether either opponent represents a particular danger. Further, how an adverse break will affect the issue. In this
case declarer is anxious to avoid East obtaining the lead since a
spade through his A10 at trick three could be disastrous.
Declarer must particularly guard against ♣A10xx with East. If
West has the clubs no harm will be done since he cannot continue the attack in spades without conceding an extra trick. Note
how declarer switches the timing by playing a heart at trick four
of the knave of clubs is allowed to win.

51. Game all; dealer South.　Contract: 6H by South.

♠ 6 4 3
♡ K 10 5 3
◇ A Q J
♣ A Q 5

♠ A K 2
♡ A 9 6 4 2
◇ K 4 3
♣ J 10

The bidding

S	N
1♡	3♣
3NT	4♡
4♠	5◇
6♡	

West leads the knave of spades. How should South plan the play?

51. Game all; dealer South.   Contract: 6H by South.

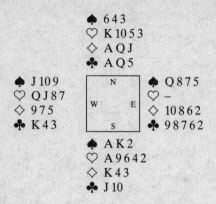

```
              ♠ 6 4 3
              ♡ K 10 5 3
              ◇ A Q J
              ♣ A Q 5
   ♠ J 10 9      N      ♠ Q 8 7 5
   ♡ Q J 8 7          ♡ –
   ◇ 9 7 5    W    E   ◇ 10 8 6 2
   ♣ K 4 3      S      ♣ 9 8 7 6 2
              ♠ A K 2
              ♡ A 9 6 4 2
              ◇ K 4 3
              ♣ J 10
```

The play
South should win the spade lead and immediately take the club
finesse. If it is wrong he will have to rely on a favourable trump
break. If it is right he can afford the luxury of a safety play in
trumps – i.e. play a small heart from either hand and if the next
player follows low cover with the nine or ten, thus ensuring that
there will be no more than one trump loser even if they break
4-0.

The principle
When there are two important issues to be resolved it is necessary to get the priorities right since the result of one may rad-
ically affect the handling of the other. In the above case South
cannot determine how to play the trump suit – to take the safety
play or not – until he knows whether he has a club loser.

52. E-W game; dealer West.   Contract: 4H by South.

♠ 9 8 5
♡ 10 3
♢ A K 10 6 4
♣ K 7 3

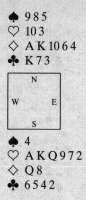

♠ 4
♡ A K Q 9 7 2
♢ Q 8
♣ 6 5 4 2

The bidding

S	W	N	E
—	Pass	Pass	Pass
1♡	Pass	2♢	2♠
3♡	3♠	4♡	Pass
Pass	Pass		

West starts with the ace and king of spades, South ruffing the second trick. Two top hearts disclose a nasty break when East throws the knave of clubs on the second round. How should declarer continue?

Playing with the odds

52. E-W game; dealer West.   Contract: 4H by South.

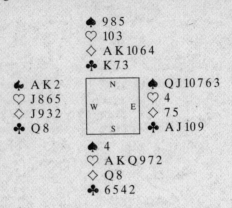

```
              ♠ 9 8 5
              ♡ 10 3
              ◇ A K 10 6 4
              ♣ K 7 3
  ♠ A K 2          N          ♠ Q J 10 7 6 3
  ♡ J 8 6 5                   ♡ 4
  ◇ J 9 3 2    W       E      ◇ 7 5
  ♣ Q 8            S          ♣ A J 10 9
              ♠ 4
              ♡ A K Q 9 7 2
              ◇ Q 8
              ♣ 6 5 4 2
```

The play
Declarer should draw a third round of trumps, cash the ◇Q and then play his last diamond towards dummy, inserting the ten when West plays low. When the ten holds, he discards two clubs on the ◇AK and disposes of a third club on the long diamond. West ruffs but the defence make only three tricks.

The principle
Confronted with a bad break in one suit it is necessary to consider how another suit must be divided if it is to restore the balance in declarer's favour. In the above case South's only hope lay with diamonds. To succeed he must obtain two discards before West ruffs. This presupposes that West will have four diamonds. Where one hand has four and the other only two, the finesse becomes mandatory.

Defence

Everyone agrees that defence is the most difficult part of the game. Perhaps that accounts for its tantalizing fascination. Although half the battle is won when your own defence improves, technical merit alone is insufficient. A further hurdle remains; it is called *partner*. Only time, and possibly bitter experience, will tell you whether it is better to rely on his signals and cooperation or form your own assessment of the position, and act on that.

Contents

1. Game all; dealer West.   Contract: 4S by South.

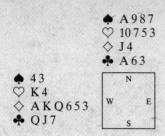

♠ A 9 8 7
♡ 10 7 5 3
◇ J 4
♣ A 6 3

♠ 4 3
♡ K 4
◇ A K Q 6 5 3
♣ Q J 7

The bidding

S	W	N	E
—	1◇	Pass	Pass
2♠	Pass	4♠	Pass
Pass	Pass		

West leads the two top diamonds, East contributing the two and seven and South the nine and ten. West then switches to a trump. Declarer draws trumps in two rounds, East throwing the two of hearts on the second one, and continues with the five of clubs from his hand. How should West plan the defence?

115

Unblocking to avoid being end-played

1. Game all; dealer West.   Contract: 4S by South.

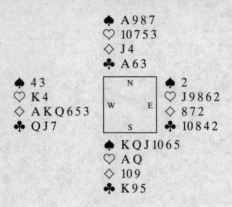

```
                    ♠ A 9 8 7
                    ♡ 10 7 5 3
                    ♢ J 4
                    ♣ A 6 3
    ♠ 4 3                           ♠ 2
    ♡ K 4                           ♡ J 9 8 6 2
    ♢ A K Q 6 5 3                   ♢ 8 7 2
    ♣ Q J 7                         ♣ 10 8 4 2
                    ♠ K Q J 10 6 5
                    ♡ A Q
                    ♢ 10 9
                    ♣ K 9 5
```

The defence

West should follow with a club honour. Declarer wins with
dummy's ace and returns a club to his hand. West must unblock
again by throwing his remaining club honour. East will eventually obtain the lead with the ♣10 to play a heart and defeat the
contract (2 diamonds, 1 club and 1 heart). If West fails to
unblock his club honours he will find himself thrown in to lead
away from the ♡K or concede a ruff and discard, which will give
declarer his tenth trick. Of course, West cannot be sure that his
partner holds the ♣10, but as both the bidding and East's
discard suggest that declarer has the ♡AQ this is the only
realistic hope.

The principle

When you foresee that you may be thrown in to make a lead
favourable to the declarer, consider unblocking. If you sacrifice
your high cards it is always possible that your partner will be the
beneficiary. The effect will be to get you off the hook and allow
him to play through the strong hand.

2. Game all; dealer North.   Contract: 4H by South.

                    ♠ 7 5 4
                    ♡ 5 2
                    ◇ 6 3 2
                    ♣ A K Q 10 9
♠ A Q J 10 8 6   ┌──────────┐
♡ A 8 4   │   N   │
◇ Q 10   │ W   E │
♣ 5 3   │   S   │
                     └──────────┘

The bidding

S	W	N	E
—	—	Pass	Pass
1♡	2♠	3♣	Pass
4♡	Pass	Pass	Pass

West leads the ace of spades, East plays the two and declarer the king. How should West plan the defence?

Cutting off the dummy

2. Game all; dealer North.   Contract: 4H by South.

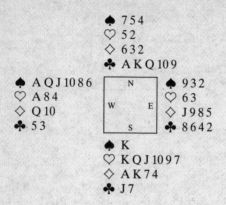

```
                      ♠ 7 5 4
                      ♡ 5 2
                      ♢ 6 3 2
                      ♣ A K Q 10 9
   ♠ A Q J 10 8 6      N        ♠ 9 3 2
   ♡ A 8 4                      ♡ 6 3
   ♢ Q 10        W         E    ♢ J 9 8 5
   ♣ 5 3              S         ♣ 8 6 4 2
                      ♠ K
                      ♡ K Q J 10 9 7
                      ♢ A K 7 4
                      ♣ J 7
```

The defence
West should switch to a club at trick two, and East should start
an echo to show four. Declarer will knock out the ♡A, and
West, on lead once more, must play a second club. Declarer may
play a third round of clubs, discarding a diamond, but West ruffs
and then can relax as the contract is now doomed. Declarer loses
1 spade, 1 heart, 1 ruff and 1 diamond.

The principle
When dummy has a long, strong suit and no outside entries,
consider attacking that suit to destroy declarer's communications. This form of defence is especially potent when you are
confident of secondary winners in the other suits. The bidding in
the above example suggests that South holds both the ace and
king of diamonds.

3. Love all; dealer North. Contract: 4S bySouth.

                    ♠ A 6 2
                    ♡ A K Q
                    ♢ A K Q
                    ♣ 9 7 4 3

    ♠ K 9 3   N
    ♡ J 7 3
    ♢ 8 4   W   E
    ♣ A K Q 10 6   S

The bidding

        N   S
        2NT   3♠
        4♢   4♠
        Pass

West cashes the three top clubs, East throwing a small heart and a small diamond on the second and third rounds. How should West plan the defence?

The uppercut

3. Love all; dealer North.   Contract: 4S by South.

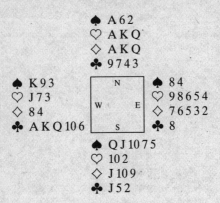

```
              ♠ A 6 2
              ♡ A K Q
              ◇ A K Q
              ♣ 9 7 4 3
  ♠ K 9 3        N        ♠ 8 4
  ♡ J 7 3               ♡ 9 8 6 5 4
  ◇ 8 4      W     E     ◇ 7 6 5 3 2
  ♣ A K Q 10 6    S      ♣ 8
              ♠ Q J 10 7 5
              ♡ 10 2
              ◇ J 10 9
              ♣ J 5 2
```

The defence
West should continue with the ♣6 at trick four, and East should ruff it with the ♠8. South overruffs with the ten, but now West's vulnerable trump holding suddenly produces a trick.

The principle
When there are no extra tricks to be won from the side suits, consider the possibility of obtaining an uppercut by continuing your own suit. This play may have the effect of promoting a trump trick. On the above hand, even if West makes the slightly inferior play of continuing with the ♣10, instead of the ♣6, East should still ruff high as he can see that the only chance for the defence lies in building up a trump trick.

4. Game all; dealer South.   Contract: 4S by South.

♠ 97
♡ 106
♢ A 10 7 2
♣ A K J 10 9

♠ 4 3 2
♡ Q J 9 7
♢ 8 4
♣ 7 5 4 2

The bidding

S	W	N	E
1♠	Double	Redouble	Pass
2♠	Pass	3♠	Pass
4♠	Pass	Pass	Pass

West leads the ace of hearts (A from AK). How should East plan the defence?

4. Game all; dealer South.   Contract: 4S by South.

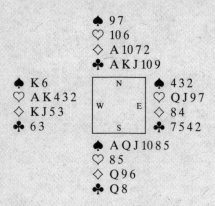

♠ 9 7
♡ 10 6
♢ A 10 7 2
♣ A K J 10 9

♠ K 6
♡ A K 4 3 2
♢ K J 5 3
♣ 6 3

♠ 4 3 2
♡ Q J 9 7
♢ 8 4
♣ 7 5 4 2

♠ A Q J 10 8 5
♡ 8 5
♢ Q 9 6
♣ Q 8

The defence
East should play the ♡Q on the ace. This requests partner to underlead his king on the next round and, of course, guarantees the knave – unless the queen is singleton. West continues with the ♡4 which East wins with the ♡J. East now switches to the ♢8, covered by the nine, knave and ace. Declarer tries the spade finesse, but West wins and cashes the ♢K. To rub it in he then gives his partner a diamond ruff. Down two.

The principle
When partner by his lead indicates the top two cards in a suit and you wish him to underplay the second, either to avoid the honours clashing or to obtain the lead, play the queen on the first card. This signal guarantees that you have the knave. In the above hand, the contract would have succeeded unless West had been able to get his partner on lead at trick two.

5. Game all; dealer South.   Contract: 4S by South.

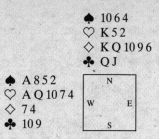

♠ 10 6 4
♥ K 5 2
♦ K Q 10 9 6
♣ Q J

♠ A 8 5 2
♥ A Q 10 7 4
♦ 7 4
♣ 10 9

The bidding

S	N
1♠	2♦
3♦	3♠
4♠	

Which card should West lead and how should he plan the defence?

The forcing game

5. Game all; dealer South.   Contract: 4S by South.

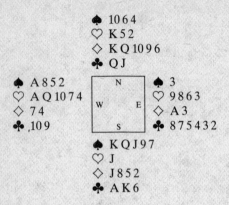

```
                    ♠ 10 6 4
                    ♡ K 5 2
                    ◇ K Q 10 9 6
                    ♣ Q J
   ♠ A 8 5 2        N           ♠ 3
   ♡ A Q 10 7 4   W   E         ♡ 9 8 6 3
   ◇ 7 4                        ◇ A 3
   ♣ 10 9            S          ♣ 8 7 5 4 3 2
                    ♠ K Q J 9 7
                    ♡ J
                    ◇ J 8 5 2
                    ♣ A K 6
```

The defence

West should lead the ♡A and continue the suit. With four
trumps to an honour West should try to weaken declarer's trump
holding. If declarer plays trumps West should withhold the ♠A
until the third round. Suppose dummy wins the second trick with
the ♡K and plays trumps. West ducks for two rounds, and now
declarer is in a quandary. If he continues with a third trump,
West wins and plays another heart. South has to ruff but he is
reduced to the same number of trumps as West and he still has to
dislodge the ◇A. Alternatively, if declarer plays a diamond
after the second round of trumps, East wins and continues
hearts. Declarer must ruff, but then when he plays a spade West
wins, and a fourth heart leaves declarer no effective counter.

The principle

When holding four trumps, especially if they are headed by an
honour or tenace, always consider a forcing defence. This
usually means attacking with your long suit. Note the ancillary
point of withholding your ace of trumps until you can exhaust
those in dummy.

6. Game all; dealer South.   Contract; 3NT by South.

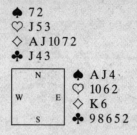

♠ 72
♡ J 5 3
♢ A J 10 7 2
♣ J 4 3

♠ A J 4
♡ 10 6 2
♢ K 6
♣ 9 8 6 5 2

The bidding

S	N
2♣	2♢
2NT	3NT

West leads the five of spades. How should East plan the defence?

6. Game all; dealer South.   Contract: 3NT by South.

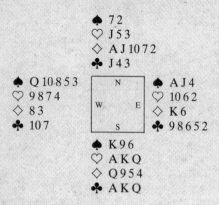

```
              ♠ 72
              ♡ J 5 3
              ◇ A J 10 7 2
              ♣ J 4 3
♠ Q 10 8 5 3         ♠ A J 4
♡ 9 8 7 4           ♡ 10 6 2
◇ 8 3               ◇ K 6
♣ 10 7              ♣ 9 8 6 5 2
              ♠ K 9 6
              ♡ A K Q
              ◇ Q 9 5 4
              ♣ A K Q
```

The defence

East should smoothly play the knave of spades, not the ace. Unaware of the spade distribution, declarer will doubtless win the ♠K and take the losing diamond finesse. The inherent risk of East's play is very small. South has advertised 23 or 24 points; there are 7 in dummy and East holds 8, so West can hold 2 points at most.

Note what happens if East makes the error of playing the ♠A on the first trick. South holds off until the third round and then can take the diamond finesse in safety.

The principle

In a no trump contract, when it is obvious that partner has no outside entry, it is good play to withhold an ace, forcing declarer to release his honour card sooner than he would have liked. This applies especially when you have a potential entry in another suit. The *locus classicus* occurs with AQx but, as we've seen in the hand above, it can sometimes be appropriate with AJx.

7. Love all; dealer South.   Contract: 3NT by South.

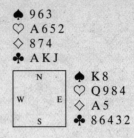

♠ 963
♡ A652
◇ 874
♣ AKJ

♠ K8
♡ Q984
◇ A5
♣ 86432

The bidding

S	N
1NT	2NT
3NT	

West leads the four of spades to East's king and South's ten. The eight of spades is returned to South's knave and West's ace. West now plays the two of spades to South's queen. How should East plan the defence?

Throwing away a high honour

7. Love all; dealer South.   Contract: 3NT by South.

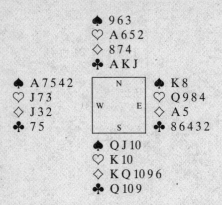

```
              ♠ 9 6 3
              ♡ A 6 5 2
              ◇ 8 7 4
              ♣ A K J

♠ A 7 5 4 2        N        ♠ K 8
♡ J 7 3                     ♡ Q 9 8 4
◇ J 3 2      W         E    ◇ A 5
♣ 7 5              S        ♣ 8 6 4 3 2

              ♠ Q J 10
              ♡ K 10
              ◇ K Q 10 9 6
              ♣ Q 10 9
```

The defence
East should jettison the ◇A on the third round of spades. That will give his partner the maximum chance of gaining an entry to enjoy the spade winners. Unless East finds this imaginative discard declarer will have no problem in making ten tricks. All he has to do is play diamonds from the dummy, twice if necessary. Once East has discarded the ◇A West's ◇J will prove an insuperable obstacle for declarer.

The principle
When partner holds winners with no apparent entry, consider discarding a high honour in a key suit to create an unexpected entry. On the above hand, had East held the ◇K instead of the ◇A it would still have been correct to jettison the high honour on the third spade.

8. Love all; dealer South.   Contract: 3NT by South.

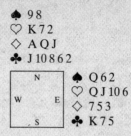

♠ 9 8
♡ K 7 2
◇ A Q J
♣ J 10 8 6 2

♠ Q 6 2
♡ Q J 10 6
◇ 7 5 3
♣ K 7 5

The bidding

S	N
1♡	2♣
2NT	3NT

West leads the five of spades to East's queen and South's four. South wins the spade continuation with the ace, West following with the three. Declarer now plays a diamond to dummy's queen and returns a small club from the table. How should East plan the defence?

8. Love all; dealer South.   Contract: 3NT by South

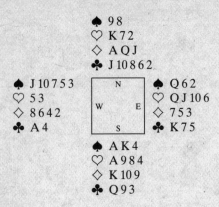

The defence

East should play the ♣K at trick four. Unless West has the ♣A there is little hope of beating the contract. Even then it is essential for East to clear the spade suit *and* preserve his partner's card of entry. When the ♣K wins and East plays a third spade, declarer will have to settle for eight tricks.

The principle

Although it is usually correct to play low second in hand ('second player plays low, third player plays high' is an oft-quoted piece of advice from the days of whist), there are many exceptions. Perhaps the most notable is when partner has a long suit and you are defending against a no trump contract. The suit is not yet established, so you must do two things: establish your partner's suit as quickly as possible, and use your own high cards for this purpose to preserve partner's card of entry. In the above hand, unless East plays the ♣K on the first round of the suit declarer will have no difficulty in making ten tricks.

9. Game all; dealer South.   Contract: 4H by South.

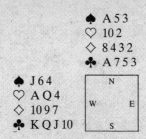

♠ A 5 3
♡ 10 2
♢ 8 4 3 2
♣ A 7 5 3

♠ J 6 4
♡ A Q 4
♢ 10 9 7
♣ K Q J 10

The bidding

S	N
1♡	1NT
3♡	4♡

West leads the king of clubs to dummy's ace, East's four and South's nine. The ten of hearts is played at trick two, East and South following with low cards. How should West plan the defence?

A little deceit

9. Game all; dealer South.   Contract: 4H by South.

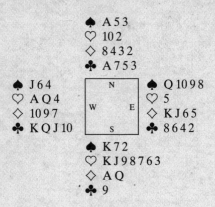

```
              ♠ A 5 3
              ♡ 10 2
              ◇ 8 4 3 2
              ♣ A 7 5 3
  ♠ J 6 4          N          ♠ Q 10 9 8
  ♡ A Q 4                     ♡ 5
  ◇ 10 9 7    W       E       ◇ K J 6 5
  ♣ K Q J 10       S          ♣ 8 6 4 2
              ♠ K 7 2
              ♡ K J 9 8 7 6 3
              ◇ A Q
              ♣ 9
```

The defence
West should win the ♡10 with the ace. This will not make any difference to the number of trump tricks the defence takes, but it will probably persuade the declarer to use his last entry to dummy to repeat the 'certain' heart finesse, rather than finesse in diamonds. The fact that South has been duped will only become apparent when it is too late for him to do anything about it.

The principle
When entries to one hand are limited, consider the effect of false carding. If this ploy deflects the declarer from taking a successful finesse, and lures him into a losing play, then your small piece of deceit will have been worth while.

10. Love all; dealer North.   Contract: 3NT by South.

♠ 5 4 3
♡ J 4
◇ A K 10 9 7 4
♣ K 4

♠ J 7
♡ Q 10 9 7 5
◇ Q 5
♣ 7 5 3 2

The bidding

S	W	N	E
—	—	1◇	1♠
2♡	Pass	3◇	Pass
3NT	Pass	Pass	Pass

West leads the knave of spades which South wins with the ace,
East following with the two. South now plays the six of
diamonds. How should West plan the defence?

10. Love all; dealer North.   Contract: 3NT by South.

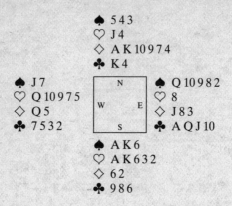

♠ 543
♡ J4
♢ A K 10 9 7 4
♣ K 4

♠ J 7
♡ Q 10 9 7 5
♢ Q 5
♣ 7 5 3 2

♠ Q 10 9 8 2
♡ 8
♢ J 8 3
♣ A Q J 10

♠ A K 6
♡ A K 6 3 2
♢ 6 2
♣ 9 8 6

The defence
West should put in the ♢Q. It cannot cost and may well upset
declarer's timing, which, in practice, is exactly what happens.
Declarer has intended ducking a diamond to East (the safe hand)
and then relying on the suit for five tricks. As it is, he cannot find
an effective counter. If he leaves West on lead he may switch to a
club, and if he takes this trick in dummy the timing and communications are broken.

The principle
Contributing a high honour as the second player often has the
effect of upsetting the timing and completely disrupting
declarer's communications. This is especially applicable when
the hand with the long suit contains no obvious outside entries.

11. Game all; dealer North.   Contract: 4H by South.

♠ K Q 10 9
♡ J 7
◇ A K Q J 3
♣ K Q

♠ 7 5 4 3 2
♡ A Q 5
◇ 7 4
♣ 10 9 8

The bidding

N	S
1D	1H
2S	3H
4H	

West leads the ten of diamonds. Dummy wins and plays the knave of hearts. How should East plan the defence?

11. Game all; dealer North.   Contract: 4H by South.

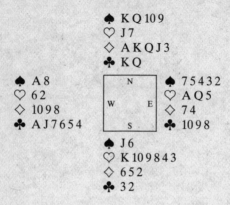

```
                        ♠ K Q 10 9
                        ♡ J 7
                        ◇ A K Q J 3
                        ♣ K Q
        ♠ A 8                              ♠ 7 5 4 3 2
        ♡ 6 2             N                ♡ A Q 5
        ◇ 10 9 8       W     E             ◇ 7 4
        ♣ A J 7 6 5 4     S                ♣ 10 9 8
                        ♠ J 6
                        ♡ K 10 9 8 4 3
                        ◇ 6 5 2
                        ♣ 3 2
```

The defence
East should duck the first round of hearts. If declarer continues
hearts (no alternative line succeeds), East should win and lock
him in the dummy with a second diamond. Now, no matter
which way he turns, declarer will be unable to prevent East
scoring his ruff. If East mistakenly wins the first heart declarer
can easily prevail by finessing East for the ♡Q.

The principle
Locking declarer in the dummy, or in his own hand, is often a
successful line of defence.The objective varies from preventing
him cashing his winners to confining him to playing from the
hand that places him at a disadvantage, or sometimes simply
delaying the moment when he can get to the hand of his choice.
An obvious example is where a defender holds the ace over
dummy's or declarer's king and refuses to release this control
until he captures the king, thereby slamming the entry gates
shut.

12. E-W game; dealer East.   Contract: 3NT by South.

♠ Q J 6
♥ 7 4
⋄ A K 5
♣ 9 8 6 5 3

♠ 9 8 7 4 3 2
♥ 6
⋄ 9 7 6 4 2
♣ K

The bidding

S	W	N	E
—	—	—	Pass
1♣	1♡	3♣	Pass
3NT	Pass	Pass	Pass

West leads the king of hearts and continues with the queen of
hearts when he is allowed to hold the first trick. How should East
plan the defence?

Throwing away a high honour

12. E-W game; dealer East.   Contract: 3NT by South.

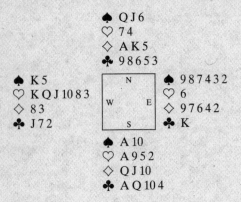

<pre>
                    ♠ Q J 6
                    ♡ 7 4
                    ◇ A K 5
                    ♣ 9 8 6 5 3
        ♠ K 5   N   ♠ 9 8 7 4 3 2
        ♡ K Q J 10 8 3   W   E   ♡ 6
        ◇ 8 3   ◇ 9 7 6 4 2
        ♣ J 7 2   S   ♣ K
                    ♠ A 10
                    ♡ A 9 5 2
                    ◇ Q J 10
                    ♣ A Q 10 4
</pre>

The defence

East should jettison his ♣K on the second round of hearts. It is
useless to him but might create an all-important entry for West.
However declarer attempts to overcome this development he
must go down. In practice he will have to play well to go only one
down (he manages this by throwing West in with a heart after
three rounds of diamonds, West having been forced to part with
one heart. West makes four hearts and one black-suit winner).
Note what can happen if East fails to discard his ♣K: declarer
enters dummy with a diamond and plays a club. When East
produces the king he is allowed to hold the trick.

The principle

When your partner is establishing a long suit but is bereft of
entries, consider throwing any high card that could create an
entry for him.

13. Love all, dealer North.   Contract: 4S by South.

♠ 9 8 7 3
♡ A Q
◇ K 7
♣ A K J 10 3

♠ A 6 4 2
♡ 10 7 3
◇ A Q J 9 4
♣ 5

The bidding

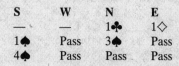

S	W	N	E
—	—	1♣	1◇
1♠	Pass	3♠	Pass
4♠	Pass	Pass	Pass

West leads his fourth highest diamond, the two, and East takes the first two tricks with the knave and ace. How should East plan the defence?

13. Love all; dealer North.   Contract: 4S by South.

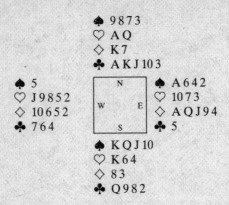

♠ 9873
♡ A Q
♦ K 7
♣ A K J 10 3

♠ 5
♡ J 9 8 5 2
♦ 10 6 5 2
♣ 7 6 4

N
W   E
S

♠ A 6 4 2
♡ 10 7 3
♦ A Q J 9 4
♣ 5

♠ K Q J 10
♡ K 6 4
♦ 8 3
♣ Q 9 8 2

The defence
Perhaps North should have tried to play in no trumps from his side of the table. As it happens that would have been a successful move, but we are concerned with four spades by South. It should be obvious to East that a ruff and discard will not benefit declarer as he can hardly have any losers in the side suits. Furthermore, if he holds only four spades his trump control is insecure. East should, therefore, play a third round of diamonds. Now, provided East withholds his ace of trumps until the third round, declarer must fail.

The principle
When you hold four trumps to the ace it is frequently correct to play a forcing game. When there are no tricks available from the side suits the best defence often lies in the deliberate concession of a ruff and discard.

14. Game all; dealer South.   Contract: 4S by South.

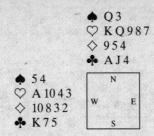

```
              ♠ Q 3
              ♡ K Q 9 8 7
              ◇ 9 5 4
              ♣ A J 4
  ♠ 5 4          N
  ♡ A 10 4 3
  ◇ 10 8 3 2   W       E
  ♣ K 7 5         S
```

The bidding

S	N
1♠	2♡
2♠	4♠

West leads the two of diamonds and notes that North's jump to four spades is exaggerated. East wins the first two diamond tricks with the king and the ace and continues with a third diamond to South's queen. South now plays the five of hearts. How should West plan the defence, and would it make any difference if he *knew* that South's heart was a singleton?

Going to bed with an ace

14. Game all; dealer South.   Contract: 4S by South.

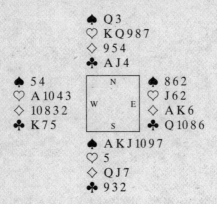

```
                        ♠ Q 3
                        ♡ K Q 9 8 7
                        ◇ 9 5 4
                        ♣ A J 4
        ♠ 5 4              N            ♠ 8 6 2
        ♡ A 10 4 3                      ♡ J 6 2
        ◇ 10 8 3 2      W       E       ◇ A K 6
        ♣ K 7 5            S            ♣ Q 10 8 6
                        ♠ A K J 10 9 7
                        ♡ 5
                        ◇ Q J 7
                        ♣ 9 3 2
```

The defence
It is quite possible that South holds a singleton heart, but even if
West is certain of this he should not contribute the ace. If he
does, that will be the end of the defence. Having ducked the
heart West will not be able to recover this trick, but there is
ample compensation when the defence make two club tricks to
defeat the contract.

The principle
There is no firm rule to cover this situation. If the loss of one
trick means that two may materialize later, it is usually best to
duck. Taking the heart situation in isolation, KQ987 opposite
the 5, there is no doubt that if West plays the ace on the first
round, catching thin air, dummy makes two tricks. But if the ace
is withheld dummy makes one trick. That is the point to which a
defender should direct his attention.

142

15. Game all; dealer South.   Contract: 3S by South.

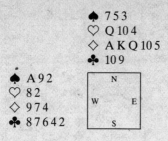

♠ 753
♡ Q 10 4
◇ A K Q 10 5
♣ 10 9

♠ A 9 2
♡ 8 2
◇ 9 7 4
♣ 8 7 6 4 2

The bidding

S	W	N	E
1♠	Pass	2◇	2♡
2♠	Pass	3♠	Pass
Pass	Pass		

West leads the eight of hearts. East wins with the knave of hearts and continues with the king and ace. South ruffs the third round with the ten of spades. How should West plan the defence?

Rejecting the overruff

15. Game all; dealer South.   Contract: 3S by South.

```
              ♠ 7 5 3
              ♡ Q 10 4
              ◇ A K Q 10 5
              ♣ 10 9
 ♠ A 9 2          N          ♠ 4
 ♡ 8 2      W         E      ♡ A K J 9 7 5
 ◇ 9 7 4                     ◇ 6 3 2
 ♣ 8 7 6 4 2      S          ♣ A 5 3
              ♠ K Q J 10 8 6
              ♡ 6 3
              ◇ J 8
              ♣ K Q J
```

The defence
West should decline to overruff, establishing the setting for a
trump promotion. When South plays a trump honour, West wins
and plays the ♣8 (signifying no interest in the suit) to his
partner's ace. East now plays a fourth round of hearts, and West,
who holds ♠92 over declarer's QJ86, must make one more
trump trick. So the defence make 2 hearts, 1 club and 2 trumps –
one down.

The principle
Do not be in a hurry to overruff if there is a chance of better
things. Sometimes an intermediate card, like an 8 or 9, will
become promoted if the defender retains his top trump. In the
above hand, had West overruffed the ♠10 declarer would have
made his contract. Say East wins the next trick with the ♣A and
continues hearts. South can now afford to ruff high and draw
trumps without hindrance.

Another position where it is invariably wrong to overruff is
when a defender holds the A10x over declarer's KQJ. If declarer
ruffs with one of his top honours the defender will make two
trump tricks if he refuses to overruff.

16. E-W game; dealer South.   Contract: 4S by South.

♠ Q 10 4
♡ 7 4
♢ A K Q 9 7
♣ J 10 9

♠ J 9 8
♡ J 8 3
♢ J 8 5 2
♣ 8 7 3

The bidding

S	W	N	E
1♠	2♡	3♢	Pass
3♠	Pass	4♠	Pass
Pass	Pass		

West leads the two top hearts. How should East plan the defence?

The false peter

16. E-W game; dealer South.   Contract: 4S by South.

                    ♠ Q 10 4
                    ♡ 7 4
                    ◇ A K Q 9 7
                    ♣ J 10 9

    ♠ 2   ♠ J 9 8
    ♡ A K Q 10 9   ♡ J 8 3
    ◇ 4 3   ◇ J 8 5 2
    ♣ A 6 5 4 2   ♣ 8 7 3

                    ♠ A K 7 6 5 3
                    ♡ 6 5 2
                    ◇ 10 6
                    ♣ K Q

The defence

East should start a peter on the first round of hearts by playing
the knave, and complete it on the second round by playing the
three. West will no doubt read this as a doubleton and continue
the suit. Declarer may now decide that his best play is to ruff
with the ♠Q (he still has several chances of success even if the
trumps are divided 3-1). If he does adopt this line, he cannot
recover and will come to no more than nine tricks.

The principle

Even if it entails giving partner false information, it is sometimes
profitable to lay a false trail by signalling a distribution that does
not exist. On the above hand, East should envisage the possibility of gaining a trump trick if declarer can be misled. Success
cannot be guaranteed (West might have six hearts), but the plan
is worth trying. Even if East had a singleton spade this ploy could
work – he would then be hoping to make an extra trump trick for
his partner. Another situation that offers scope for chicanery is
when the suit is divided like this:

                    Q 10 9 3
            A K 5   ☐   J 8 4
                    7 3 2

On the ace East plays the eight. He then completes the peter
with the four on the king. Suspecting a doubleton, declarer may
play the ten on the next round.

17. Game all; dealer South.   Contract: 6S by South.

```
                    ♠ 7 3
                    ♡ 6 3 2
                    ◇ A K Q 9 5
                    ♣ J 6 3
                             ♠ 9 2
             N               ♡ 9 7 5
       W           E         ◇ 1 0 7 3 2
             S               ♣ K 1 0 7 4
```

The bidding

S	N
2♣	3◇
4♠	5◇
5♡	5♠
6♠	

West leads the queen of hearts to South's ace. At trick two South
plays the eight of spades, West following with the four and
dummy with the three. How should East plan the defence?

Refusing a Greek gift

17. Game all; dealer South. Contract: 6S by South.

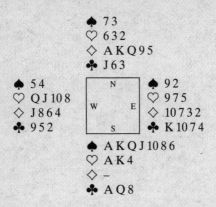

♠ 73
♥ 632
♦ A K Q 9 5
♣ J 6 3

♠ 54
♥ Q J 10 8
♦ J 8 6 4
♣ 9 5 2

♠ 92
♥ 9 7 5
♦ 10 7 3 2
♣ K 10 7 4

♠ A K Q J 10 8 6
♥ A K 4
♦ –
♣ A Q 8

The defence
East must refuse this Greek gift. It should be obvious that
declarer's trump suit is solid, so that his only reason for playing a
low one is to gain an entry to dummy. It follows that declarer is
void in diamonds. If, later in the game, he plays the ♣Q East
must refuse this trick as well. As a last resort declarer will
probably play off all his trumps, hoping for a careless discard or
an end-play. In practice the discards are easy. The diamonds are
expendable and each player can let go one club. The result of
this careful defence will be one down.

The principle
Good bridge players are not renowned for their philanthropy, so
when an expert offers you a present it is usually best to reject it.
At least try to perceive the reason for his generosity before you
accept it. In the above hand South was desperate to get to
dummy, and he had to hope that either the ♠9 was singleton or
one of his opponents would make an error.

18. N-S game; dealer South.   Contract: 4S by South.

♠ Q 2
♡ J 7 4
◇ A K J 10 8 6
♣ Q 8

N	
W E	
S	

♠ A 5 3
♡ 9 5
◇ 9 3
♣ A K J 9 6 5

The bidding

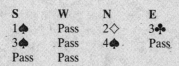

S	W	N	E
1♠	Pass	2◇	3♣
3♠	Pass	4♠	Pass
Pass	Pass		

West leads the two of clubs. East wins the first two tricks in the suit, South following with the four and seven and West with the three. How should East plan the defence?

149

Cutting off the dummy

18. N-S game; dealer South.   Contract: 4S by South.

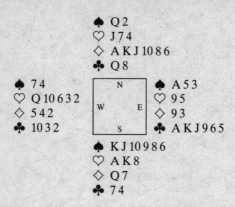

```
                    ♠ Q 2
                    ♡ J 7 4
                    ◇ A K J 10 8 6
                    ♣ Q 8
    ♠ 7 4              N          ♠ A 5 3
    ♡ Q 10 6 3 2                 ♡ 9 5
    ◇ 5 4 2        W      E       ◇ 9 3
    ♣ 10 3 2          S          ♣ A K J 9 6 5
                    ♠ K J 10 9 8 6
                    ♡ A K 8
                    ◇ Q 7
                    ♣ 7 4
```

The defence
On the bidding it is likely that South holds both the ace and king
of hearts, so East's best chance is to try and cut declarer off from
the dummy. A diamond switch at trick three will set the wheels
in motion. South wins the diamond in his own hand and plays the
knave of spades. East ducks (an essential counter), wins the
spade continuation and plays a second diamond, eclipsing the
dummy completely. The declarer will probably try for a discard,
but East scotches that plan with his ♠5. Eventually West will
make his ♡Q for one down.

The principle
Killing the dummy by playing dummy's long suit is a ploy that
can often be exploited when dummy has no outside cards of
entry especially if there is no side suit that can be profitably
attacked.

19. Love all; dealer South.　　Contract: 6S by South.

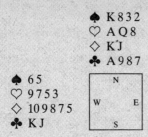

♠ K 8 3 2
♡ A Q 8
◇ K J
♣ A 9 8 7

♠ 6 5
♡ 9 7 5 3
◇ 1 0 9 8 7 5
♣ K J

```
      N
  W       E
      S
```

The bidding

S	N
1♠	3♣
3♠	4♠
5◇	5♡
6♠	

West leads the ten of diamonds to dummy's knave, East's three
and South's queen. Declarer draws trumps in two rounds and
plays the ace of clubs. How should West plan the defence?

Unblocking

19. Love all; dealer South.   Contract: 6S by South.

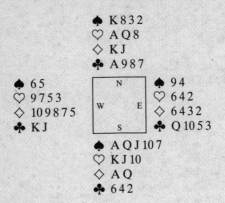

```
              ♠ K 8 3 2
              ♡ A Q 8
              ◇ K J
              ♣ A 9 8 7
   ♠ 6 5                      ♠ 9 4
   ♡ 9 7 5 3                  ♡ 6 4 2
   ◇ 10 9 8 7 5               ◇ 6 4 3 2
   ♣ K J                      ♣ Q 10 5 3
              ♠ A Q J 10 7
              ♡ K J 10
              ◇ A Q
              ♣ 6 4 2
```

The defence
West should disembarrass himself of the ♣K. If he fails to do
this declarer will eliminate the red suits and play a second club.
West will now be end-played and have to concede a ruff and
discard.

The principle
When an end-play looms, consider unblocking to avoid being
thrown on lead to declarer's advantage. Kx is a dangerous holding in this sort of setting. In the above example it is almost
inconceivable that the unblock will cost the contract. In practice
it is the only defence.

20. N-S game; dealer South.   Contract: 4H by South.

                    ♠ K Q J 9
                    ♡ 4
                    ♢ 7 6 2
                    ♣ A K J 10 9
    ♠ 5 2
    ♡ A 8 3   N
    ♢ A K Q 10 8 5   W   E
    ♣ 6 4   S

The bidding

S	W	N	E
1♡	3♢	4♣	Pass
4♡	Pass	Pass	Pass

West leads the queen of diamonds on which East plays the nine and South the three. How should West plan the defence?

The uppercut

20. N-S game; dealer South.   Contract: 4H by South.

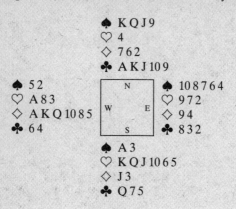

```
                  ♠ K Q J 9
                  ♡ 4
                  ◇ 7 6 2
                  ♣ A K J 10 9
     ♠ 5 2                          ♠ 10 8 7 6 4
     ♡ A 8 3            N           ♡ 9 7 2
     ◇ A K Q 10 8 5   W   E         ◇ 9 4
     ♣ 6 4                          ♣ 8 3 2
                         S
                  ♠ A 3
                  ♡ K Q J 10 6 5
                  ◇ J 3
                  ♣ Q 7 5
```

The defence

West should cash the ◇A (East's nine signifies that he holds no
more than a doubleton) and then play a low diamond. With the
◇K marked in West's hand, East should have no difficulty in
recognizing that he should ruff high (this might well be the best
play with a less erudite partner who simply played out the three
top diamonds). The ♡9 forces declarer to overruff with the
♡10. Then when West wins with the ♡A he plays a fourth
diamond. East's ♡7 is taken by South's ♡J, but this second
uppercut promotes West's ♡8 to master rank after the declarer
has cashed the ♡Q.

The principle

When it is obvious that there are no more tricks to be taken from
the side suits a defender should focus his attention on the trump
suit. On the above hand West can see 27 points and can infer that
declarer will have virtually all the remainder to justify his
opening bid. The only hope is that East will have sufficiently
powerful trump intermediates to promote West's ♡8 to winning
rank.

21. Game all; dealer South.   Contract: 3NT by South.

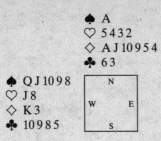

```
                    ♠ A
                    ♡ 5 4 3 2
                    ◇ A J 10 9 5 4
                    ♣ 6 3
     ♠ Q J 10 9 8      ┌─────────┐
     ♡ J 8             │    N    │
     ◇ K 3             │ W     E │
     ♣ 10 9 8 5        │    S    │
                       └─────────┘
```

The bidding

S	N
1♣	1◇
1♠	2◇
2NT	3NT

West leads the queen of spades to dummy's ace, East playing the two. Declarer enters his hand with the ace of hearts and leads a low diamond. How should West play the defence?

Disrupting communications

21. Game all; dealer South.   Contract: 3NT by South.

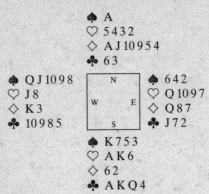

```
                        ♠ A
                        ♡ 5 4 3 2
                        ◇ A J 10 9 5 4
                        ♣ 6 3
        ♠ Q J 10 9 8         N         ♠ 6 4 2
        ♡ J 8                           ♡ Q 10 9 7
        ◇ K 3          W         E      ◇ Q 8 7
        ♣ 10 9 8 5          S          ♣ J 7 2
                        ♠ K 7 5 3
                        ♡ A K 6
                        ◇ 6 2
                        ♣ A K Q 4
```

The defence

West must play the ◇K on the first round, presenting declarer with an insoluble problem. Declarer can duck, and then perhaps try the finesse on the next round, in which case he won't take a diamond trick at all. Alternatively, he can win with the ace, which leaves East in control. Sensing that two diamond tricks may be enough for the contract, East can win the second round (in any case he is quite safe as long as South has no more than a doubleton) and now South can wave goodbye to his game. There were eight tricks on top originally and declarer's prospects have not improved now that the diamond suit has been rendered inaccessible.

The principle

Be prepared to play an honour card if by so doing you disrupt the enemy communications. In the above hand it is most unlikely to cost if you go up with the ◇K on the first round; if South has a doubleton it is likely to destroy his prospects entirely. If West had ◇K73 and East Q8 it would still be right for West to contribute the king on the first round. Now declarer has a guess. If an inexpert West fails to play the king, East should duck. On this hand declarer has enough to spare; on another occasion it might be crucial.

156

22. E-W game; dealer North.   Contract: 3H by South.

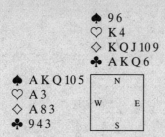

♠ 9 6
♡ K 4
♢ K Q J 10 9
♣ A K Q 6

♠ A K Q 10 5
♡ A 3
♢ A 8 3
♣ 9 4 3

N
W   E
S

The bidding

S	W	N	E
—	—	1♢	Pass
1♡	1♠	2♣	Pass
2♡	2♠	3♡	Pass
Pass	Pass		

West leads the ace of spades, East following with the two and South the three. How should West plan the defence?

Controlling the trump suit

22. E-W game; dealer North.   Contract: 3H by South.

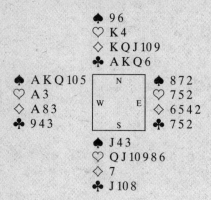

♠ 9 6
♡ K 4
◇ K Q J 10 9
♣ A K Q 6

♠ A K Q 10 5   ♠ 8 7 2
♡ A 3   ♡ 7 5 2
◇ A 8 3   ◇ 6 5 4 2
♣ 9 4 3   ♣ 7 5 2

♠ J 4 3
♡ Q J 10 9 8 6
◇ 7
♣ J 10 8

The defence
West should play the ♡3 at trick two. Whatever declarer does now, West is in command and the contract must fail. If declarer plays a second spade, West wins and cashes the ♡A, a third spade and the ◇A. If declarer plays a diamond, West wins and cashes the ♡A and two more spade tricks. Note that no other defence will defeat the contract.

The principle
When it is obligatory to retain control of the trump suit, consider playing low from Ax, or Axx. This advice applies especially when there are precisely two trumps in the dummy.

23. Game all; dealer North.   Contract: 4S by South.

♠ Q 8 5 3
♡ Q
♢ K J 10 7 4
♣ A J 7

♠ K J 10
♡ A K 10 8 4
♢ A 6 3
♣ 10 9

The bidding

S	W	N	E
—	—	1♢	Pass
1♠	2♡	2♠	Pass
3♡	Pass	4♠	Pass
Pass	Pass		

West leads a top heart and switches to the ten of clubs. Declarer wins in his hand with the king while East follows with the two. Declarer then cashes the ace of spades. How should West plan the defence?

Laying a false trail

23. Game all; dealer North.   Contract: 4S by South.

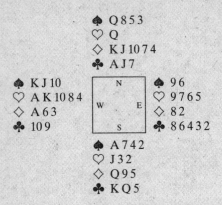

```
                    ♠ Q 8 5 3
                    ♡ Q
                    ◇ K J 10 7 4
                    ♣ A J 7
   ♠ K J 10          ┌─────────┐        ♠ 9 6
   ♡ A K 10 8 4      │    N    │        ♡ 9 7 6 5
   ◇ A 6 3        W  │         │  E      ◇ 8 2
   ♣ 10 9           │    S    │        ♣ 8 6 4 3 2
                    └─────────┘
                    ♠ A 7 4 2
                    ♡ J 3 2
                    ◇ Q 9 5
                    ♣ K Q 5
```

The defence
West should drop the king of spades on the ace! It can't cost.
Declarer obviously plans to draw trumps, and when he plays a
low one towards the queen the defenders will make only one
trump trick. However, the play of the king under the ace may
persuade the declarer to postpone drawing trumps for fear of
losing control of the hand should East hold the ◇A and SJ1096.
Declarer may decide to knock out the ◇A before playing any
more spades. Once again West must be on his toes: he ducks the
first round, wins the second and hammers the last nail in the
coffin by giving East a ruff.

The principle
When all seems lost, it is well worth trying an extravagant play if
it might lead declarer astray. In the above example West should
see that he can never make more than one trump, no matter
which card he plays on the ace.

24. Love all; dealer South.   Contract: 4H by South.

♠ J 6 3
♡ 7 4
◇ K Q J 10 9
♣ A J 5

        ♠ Q 9 5
        ♡ J 8 3 2
        ◇ A 7
        ♣ 8 6 3 2

The bidding

S	W	N	E
1♡	1♠	2◇	2♠
3♡	Pass	4♡	Pass
Pass	Pass		

West leads the ace and king of spades and switches to the ten of clubs. South wins with the king, cashes the ace and king of hearts, West discarding a spade on the second round, and plays the six of diamonds to dummy's king and East's ace, West following with the two. How should East plan the defence?

24. Love all; dealer South.   Contract: 4H by South.

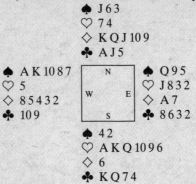

♠ J 6 3
♡ 7 4
♢ K Q J 10 9
♣ A J 5

♠ A K 10 8 7
♡ 5
♢ 8 5 4 3 2
♣ 10 9

♠ Q 9 5
♡ J 8 3 2
♢ A 7
♣ 8 6 3 2

♠ 4 2
♡ A K Q 10 9 6
♢ 6
♣ K Q 7 4

The defence

East must return a club at trick five. If he plays any other suit
declarer will make his contract, as he will have the entries to
reduce his trumps (two ruffs are needed) to the same number as
East's. Declarer will then be able to finish in the dummy and play
diamonds with the ♡Q10 poised over East's ♡J8. Without
East's assistance, however, it will be impossible for South to
shorten his trumps *and* finish in dummy to coup East. Suppose
East returns a spade: South will ruff, enter dummy with a club
and ruff a diamond. Finally dummy is re-entered with the last
club, and diamonds are played until East surrenders. Note that
West played well by refusing to continue with a third spade. It
was obvious that declarer had no more spades, and West's
singleton heart suggested the possibility of a bad trump break. In
such circumstances it can be fatal to help declarer reduce his
trumps. East could be certain that this was the case – West could
infer it.

The principle

When there is a possibility of declarer's wishing to trump coup
one of his opponents, do not help him to reduce his trumps. The
best defence lies in attacking his entries – as in the above
example.

25. Love all; dealer South.   Contract: 4H by South.

♠ Q 10 7 5
♡ K 10 9 7
♢ K J 10
♣ K Q

           ♠ A 4
           ♡ 5 2
           ♢ 9 8 6 3 2
           ♣ 9 8 6 4

The bidding

S	N
1NT	2♣
2♡	4♡

West leads the ace of diamonds – A,10,8,4 – and in response to East's eight continues with the seven of diamonds. How should East plan the defence?

25. Love all; dealer South. Contract: 4H by South.

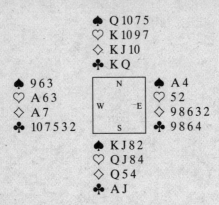

♠ Q 10 7 5
♡ K 10 9 7
♢ K J 10
♣ K Q

♠ 9 6 3
♡ A 6 3
♢ A 7
♣ 10 7 5 3 2

N
W E
S

♠ A 4
♡ 5 2
♢ 9 8 6 3 2
♣ 9 8 6 4

♠ K J 8 2
♡ Q J 8 4
♢ Q 5 4
♣ A J

The defence
It is obvious that West is looking for a diamond ruff, so East
encourages the plan by playing the ♢8. When West continues
with a second diamond East should continue his collaboration by
following with the ♢9 to indicate his card of entry, the ♠A. If
East holds the ♣A, instead of the ♠A, he should follow to the
second diamond with the two. In the above hand, when West
wins with the ♡A he will switch to a spade and the diamond
return will defeat the contract.

The principle
When one defender embarks on an unmistakable line of defence
it is his partner's duty to assist him. On the above hand East's
high diamond suggests a liking for the ruffing plan, and his ♢9
indicates the entry. There are many opportunities for the
McKenney suit preference signal to indicate where the entry lies.

26. Game all; dealer North.   Contract: 4S by South.

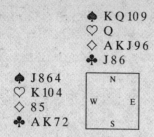

♠ K Q 10 9
♥ Q
♦ A K J 9 6
♣ J 8 6

♠ J 8 6 4
♥ K 10 4
♦ 8 5
♣ A K 7 2

The bidding

N	S
1♦	1♠
3♠	4♠

West leads the ace of clubs and, encouraged by his partner's nine, continues with the king and another. East wins the third round with the queen and switches to the five of hearts, won by declarer's ace. Declarer now plays the three of spades towards dummy. How should West plan the defence?

The obligatory false card

26. Game all; dealer North.   Contract: 4S by South.

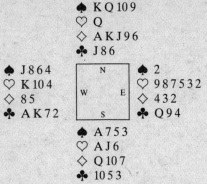

```
                  ♠ K Q 10 9
                  ♡ Q
                  ◇ A K J 9 6
                  ♣ J 8 6
    ♠ J 8 6 4         N         ♠ 2
    ♡ K 10 4                    ♡ 9 8 7 5 3 2
    ◇ 8 5          W     E      ◇ 4 3 2
    ♣ A K 7 2         S         ♣ Q 9 4
                  ♠ A 7 5 3
                  ♡ A J 6
                  ◇ Q 10 7
                  ♣ 10 5 3
```

The defence

West should follow with the ♠8, dummy's king winning the tricks. If the spades are divided 4-4-4-1 South will have to guess which defender is more likely to hold Jxxx. The eight on the first round from West may persuade the declarer that East is more likely to hold length than his partner. If the declarer plays the queen of spades next there is no way to recover.

The principle

When declarer may have a guess in a suit a false card may persuade him to follow a losing line. In the above hand the declarer might have gone wrong in any case, but West's ♠8 should speed him to his doom. This is an analogous position:

```
            A K 10 5
    J 9 6 3    □    4
            Q 8 7 2
```

Whether South plays low towards dummy or cashes dummy's ace, West must contribute the *nine,* providing declarer with a losing option. Quite possibly declarer will continue with the king. Now the defence must make one trick in the suit. Unless West plays the nine on the first round, South will certainly play low to the queen as his next move because he can pick up J9xx with West, but not with East.

27. Love all; dealer South.   Contract: 3NT by South.

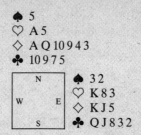

♠ 5
♡ A 5
◇ A Q 10 9 4 3
♣ 10 9 7 5

		♠ 3 2
N		♡ K 8 3
W	E	◇ K J 5
	S	♣ Q J 8 3 2

The bidding

S	N
1♠	2◇
2♡	3◇
3NT	

West leads the queen of spades to South's king. At trick two South plays the seven of diamonds, West follows with the eight, dummy the nine and East the knave. How should East plan the defence?

The Merrimac coup

27. Love all; dealer South.   Contract: 3NT by South.

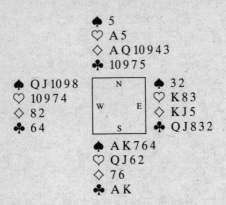

♠ 5
♡ A 5
◇ A Q 10 9 4 3
♣ 10 9 7 5

♠ Q J 10 9 8   ♠ 3 2
♡ 10 9 7 4   ♡ K 8 3
◇ 8 2   ◇ K J 5
♣ 6 4   ♣ Q J 8 3 2

♠ A K 7 6 4
♡ Q J 6 2
◇ 7 6
♣ A K

The defence

East should play the ♡K (Merrimac coup) in order to kill
dummy's entry to the diamond suit. Although declarer can now
make three quick tricks in hearts his tally in diamonds is limited
to one, the ace, and his total tricks to eight.

The principle

When dummy has only one entry to a long suit that is not yet
established, consider sacrificing a high honour (usually a king) to
kill that entry. In the above example, the ♡K at trick three is the
only card to play to defeat the contract.

28. Love all; dealer South.   Contract: 3NT by South.

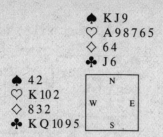

♠ K J 9
♡ A 9 8 7 6 5
♢ 6 4
♣ J 6

♠ 4 2
♡ K 10 2
♢ 8 3 2
♣ K Q 10 9 5

The bidding

S	N
1♢	1♡
1♠	2♡
2NT	3NT

West leads the king of clubs, East follows with the two and South the four. How should West plan the defence?

28. Love all; dealer South.   Contract: 3NT by South.

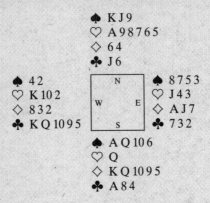

```
              ♠ K J 9
              ♡ A 9 8 7 6 5
              ◇ 6 4
              ♣ J 6
♠ 4 2              N              ♠ 8 7 5 3
♡ K 10 2                          ♡ J 4 3
◇ 8 3 2       W       E           ◇ A J 7
♣ K Q 10 9 5       S              ♣ 7 3 2
              ♠ A Q 10 6
              ♡ Q
              ◇ K Q 10 9 5
              ♣ A 8 4
```

The defence

West should continue with the ♣Q, but when he is allowed to
hold the second trick he must switch to a heart. Not any heart,
but the ♡K precisely. South has bid diamonds and spades and
presumably also holds three clubs. Probably he has a singleton
heart, which could be the queen. If the ♡K is ducked, West
continues the suit, establishing 2 clubs, 2 hearts and 1 diamond.
At the table West meekly continued with a third club. Now there
was no defence.

The principle

When planning your defence, don't pursue a line that is guaranteed to fail. If you stop and go over the bidding again it may
become obvious that you must amend your original plan. There
are clues available from most auctions and the one in the above
example was especially enlightening.

29. Game all; dealer South.   Contract: 3NT by South.

♠ A J 3
♡ 10 7 3
◇ Q 10
♣ A Q J 9 4

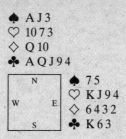

♠ 7 5
♡ K J 9 4
◇ 6 4 3 2
♣ K 6 3

The bidding

S	N
1◇	2♣
2NT	3NT

West leads the ten of spades which South wins with the king. At trick two South plays the ten of clubs, West following with the seven and dummy with the four. How should East plan the defence?

171

29. Game all; dealer South.   Contract: 3NT by South.

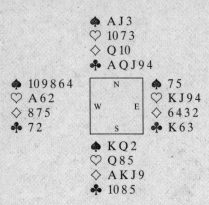

♠ A J 3
♡ 10 7 3
◇ Q 10
♣ A Q J 9 4

♠ 10 9 8 6 4   ♠ 7 5
♡ A 6 2   ♡ K J 9 4
◇ 8 7 5   ◇ 6 4 3 2
♣ 7 2   ♣ K 6 3

♠ K Q 2
♡ Q 8 5
◇ A K J 9
♣ 10 8 5

The defence
East should win with the ♣K and switch to the *knave* of hearts.
He must hope that his partner has at least ♡Axx, in which case
the contract will be defeated. The presence of the ♡10 in
dummy makes it imperative that East plays the knave. No other
card will do. Note that East cannot afford to duck the first round
of clubs because South may run for home.

The principle
There are many occasions when a player must visualize, and rely
upon, a precise holding in partner's hand to defeat the contract.
Compare the heart suit in the above example with this slightly
altered setting:

```
              10 8 7 3
        A 6 2   □   K J 9 4
              Q 5
```

In this instance East must play the king otherwise the defence
cannot cash four tricks.

30. E-W game; dealer West.   Contract: 4S by South.

♠ Q J 10 7
♡ 8
◇ K Q 9 7
♣ A K J 10

♠ 5 2
♡ K Q J 10 9 4 3 2
◇ J 10 2
♣ —

N
W   E
S

The bidding

S	W	N	E
—	3♡	Double	Pass
4♠	Pass	Pass	Pass

Which card should West lead? If East wins the first trick with the ace of hearts and returns the nine of clubs, how should West continue the defence?

30. E-W game: dealer West.   Contract: 4S by South.

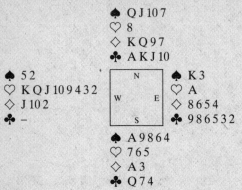

<pre>
                    ♠ Q J 10 7
                    ♡ 8
                    ◇ K Q 9 7
                    ♣ A K J 10
   ♠ 5 2   ♠ K 3
   ♡ K Q J 10 9 4 3 2   ♡ A
   ◇ J 10 2   ◇ 8 6 5 4
   ♣ —   ♣ 9 8 6 5 3 2
                    ♠ A 9 8 6 4
                    ♡ 7 6 5
                    ◇ A 3
                    ♣ Q 7 4
</pre>

The defence

As we shall see, N-S did well to stop in four spades. Wanting a club ruff, West should make the unnatural lead of the ♡2. a McKenney suit preference signal asking for a club return. East wins and, since he wants his partner to play another heart and not a diamond, he returns the ♣9. West ruffs and plays the ♡3. East overruffs dummy and sends back a second club to complete declarer's frustration. Had East held the ◇A instead of the ♠K he would have returned a low club at trick two. Equally, had West been void of diamonds instead of clubs he would have led the ♡9 originally.

The principle

Although it is rare to give a suit preference signal on the opening lead, it does happen, usually when one hand is known to hold length in a suit and then makes an unusual lead. For example, a very small card from a long suit or a 9, 8 or 7 from a suit that obviously contains several honours. The most frequent setting for this type of lead is where a player has made a jump overcall (say three diamonds over one heart) and leads either the ◇9 or ◇2 against four hearts. This strange opening lead (◇9) would surely request partner to return a spade, whereas the ◇2 would ask for a club.

31 Love all; dealer East.   Contract: 4♡ by South.

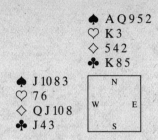

                        ♠ A Q 9 5 2
                        ♡ K 3
                        ◇ 5 4 2
                        ♣ K 8 5

        ♠ J 10 8 3
        ♡ 7 6
        ◇ Q J 10 8
        ♣ J 4 3

The bidding

S	W	N	E
—	—	—	1NT
2♡	Pass	4♡	Pass
Pass	Pass		

West leads the queen of diamonds, and the defence take three
tricks in this suit. At trick four East, who has shown ◇AK9,
switches to the ten of clubs, won by declarer's ace. The next
trick, a spade to dummy's ace, comprises the 6-3-A-4. Now
declarer returns the two of spades, which he ruffs. How should
West plan the defence?

The obligatory false card

31. Love all, dealer East.   Contract: 4H by South.

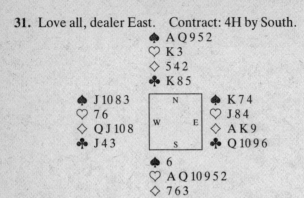

♠ A Q 9 5 2
♡ K 3
♢ 5 4 2
♣ K 8 5

♠ J 10 8 3
♡ 7 6
♢ Q J 10 8
♣ J 4 3

♠ K 7 4
♡ J 8 4
♢ A K 9
♣ Q 10 9 6

♠ 6
♡ A Q 10 9 5 2
♢ 7 6 3
♣ A 7 2

The defence

West must follow with the ♠10 on the second round. Without this obligatory false card declarer will enter dummy with the ♡K and ruff another low spade, dropping the king. He can now dispose of his club loser, making 6 hearts, 2 clubs and 2 spades. When the ♠10 appears, South may continue with the ♠Q when next he leads the suit. This play would be successful if West had started with ♠J103 originally, as the ♠Q now pins the ♠J.

The principle

If declarer is going to succeed by standard play the defence must attempt a diversion.

An analogous situation arises with this distribution:

K J 5

Q 10 6   □   8 3 2

A 9 7 4

South plays small to the knave and then cashes the king. Now West must follow with the queen, the card he is known to hold, to provide South with a false trail. Should West follow to the second round with the ten South cannot go wrong.

176

32. Love all; dealer South.　　Contract: 3NT by South.

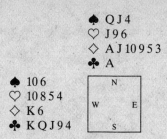

♠ Q J 4
♡ J 9 6
♢ A J 10 9 5 3
♣ A

♠ 10 6
♡ 10 8 5 4
♢ K 6
♣ K Q J 9 4

The bidding

S	N
1NT*	3♢
3NT	

(*12–14 points)

West leads the king of clubs, East following with the two. South enters his hand with the ace of hearts and plays a low diamond. How should West plan the defence?

32. Love all; dealer South.   Contract: 3NT by South.

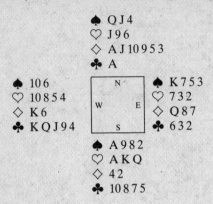

♠ Q J 4
♡ J 9 6
♢ A J 10 9 5 3
♣ A

♠ 10 6
♡ 10 8 5 4
♢ K 6
♣ K Q J 9 4

♠ K 7 5 3
♡ 7 3 2
♢ Q 8 7
♣ 6 3 2

♠ A 9 8 2
♡ A K Q
♢ 4 2
♣ 10 8 7 5

The defence
West should follow with the ♢6. If he plays the king, hoping to
disrupt the communications in the diamond suit, declarer may
decide to play for an unlikely lie of the cards which actully exists
on this occasion. He wins the ♢A and plays the ♠Q. If East fails
to cover, he continues with the ♠J, pinning the ten. He gets
home with four spades, three hearts and two minor-suit aces. If
West plays a low diamond at trick two it is probable that the
declarer will finesse. His plan will be to bring in the diamond
suit, hoping not to lose more than three clubs (the suit may be
evenly divided or East may have the 9).

The principle
Although it is often right to play an honour card in front of a long
suit, it should not be automatic. On this occasion there are other
considerations. Above all, West wants his partner on lead to play
a club. It might be difficult to envisage the danger of the spade
suit but West does not want declarer to look for an alternative
line of play.

33. N-S game; dealer North.   Contract: 3NT by South.

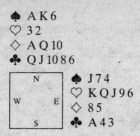

♠ A K 6
♡ 3 2
♦ A Q 10
♣ Q J 10 8 6

              N   ♠ J 7 4
                         ♡ K Q J 9 6
         W   E   ♦ 8 5
              S   ♣ A 4 3

The bidding

S	W	N	E
—	—	1♣	1♡
1NT	Pass	2NT	Pass
3NT	Pass	Pass	Pass

West leads the seven of hearts. How should East plan the defence?

Communication play

33. N-S game; dealer North.   Contract: 3NT by South.

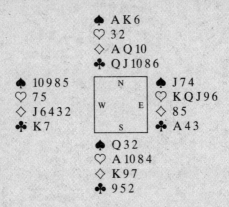

```
                    ♠ A K 6
                    ♡ 3 2
                    ◇ A Q 10
                    ♣ Q J 10 8 6
   ♠ 10 9 8 5         N          ♠ J 7 4
   ♡ 7 5                         ♡ K Q J 9 6
   ◇ J 6 4 3 2    W       E      ◇ 8 5
   ♣ K 7                         ♣ A 4 3
                     S
                    ♠ Q 3 2
                    ♡ A 10 8 4
                    ◇ K 9 7
                    ♣ 9 5 2
```

The defence
East should play the ♡9, hoping that West can get in again to
lead a second heart while East retains the ♣A. Probably South
holds ♡A10xx. If East makes the mistake of playing the ♡J
South will duck, effectively ending the defence.

The principle
If the defence to a no trump contract, if your partner leads your
suit and is obviously short in it himself, consider allowing the
declarer to win a cheap trick immediately. Then, if partner can
regain the lead, he may be able to continue your suit while you
retain your card of entry.

34. Game all; dealer North.   Contract: 3NT by South.

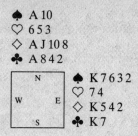

♠ A 10
♡ 6 5 3
◇ A J 10 8
♣ A 8 4 2

♠ K 7 6 3 2
♡ 7 4
◇ K 5 4 2
♣ K 7

The bidding

N	S
1◇	2♣
3♣	3NT

West leads the king of hearts followed by the queen. South plays the knave on the first round and wins the second with the ace. He continues with the queen of clubs to East's king. How should East plan the defence?

The Deschapelles coup

34. Game all; dealer North.   Contract: 3NT by South.

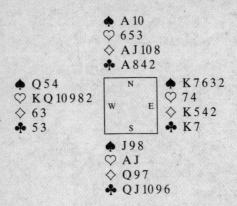

```
                    ♠ A 10
                    ♡ 6 5 3
                    ◇ A J 10 8
                    ♣ A 8 4 2
    ♠ Q 5 4              N              ♠ K 7 6 3 2
    ♡ K Q 10 9 8 2                      ♡ 7 4
    ◇ 6 3          W         E          ◇ K 5 4 2
    ♣ 5 3                               ♣ K 7
                         S
                    ♠ J 9 8
                    ♡ A J
                    ◇ Q 9 7
                    ♣ Q J 10 9 6
```

The defence

East should play the ♠K at trick four (Deschapelles coup), hoping to create an entry to West's hand. If declarer ducks, then East continues with a second spade dislodging dummy's ace. When East regains the lead with the ◇K he can put his partner in to cash the heart winners. In practice this defence is likely to hold declarer to six tricks.

The principle

When it is vital to create an entry to enable partner to cash his winners, consider sacrificing a high honour to promote partner's honour. In the above example East did not know that West held the ♠Q, but it was the best chance.

35. E-W game; dealer West.   Contract: 4H by South.

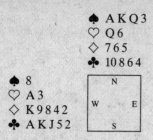

♠ A K Q 3
♡ Q 6
♢ 7 6 5
♣ 10 8 6 4

♠ 8
♡ A 3
♢ K 9 8 4 2
♣ A K J 5 2

The bidding

S	W	N	E
—	1♢	Pass	Pass
2♡	3♣	4♡	Pass
Pass	Pass		

West leads two top clubs, East following with the nine and the three and South the seven and queen. How should West continue?

35. E-W game; dealer West.   Contract: 4H by South.

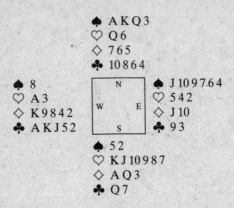

```
            ♠ A K Q 3
            ♡ Q 6
            ◇ 7 6 5
            ♣ 10 8 6 4
♠ 8                              ♠ J 10 9 7 6 4
♡ A 3            N               ♡ 5 4 2
◇ K 9 8 4 2   W     E            ◇ J 10
♣ A K J 5 2       S              ♣ 9 3
            ♠ 5 2
            ♡ K J 10 9 8 7
            ◇ A Q 3
            ♣ Q 7
```

The defence
West should play allow club at trick three (as it happens, the
knave will do no harm),and then when he is on lead with the ♡A
play the ♣J, thereby destroying dummy's club menace. Suppose
West fails to see the danger and switches to a spade. Dummy
wins and the ♡A is knocked out. It is now too late to defuse the
club suit. Declarer cashes all the trumps and the ♠KQ. Before
the last top spade is played, dummy is down to ♠Q, ◇7, ♣10.
South has ◇AQ3 and West ◇KJ, ♣J. East's holding is
immaterial. On the ♠Q South discards the ◇3, but West is in
trouble. He has either to blank his ◇K or throw away the master
club. Remembering the bidding declarer can hardly go wrong.

The principle
When a defender envisages an impending squeeze, he should try
to destroy the menace cards held against him. If he can reduce
the danger suits to one, instead of two or more, the squeeze will
be still-born.

36. Love all; dealer North.   Contract: 4S by South.

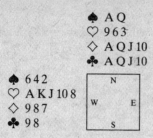

♠ A Q
♡ 9 6 3
♢ A Q J 10
♣ A Q J 10

♠ 6 4 2
♡ A K J 10 8
♢ 9 8 7
♣ 9 8

The bidding

N	S
2NT	4♠

West leads the ace of hearts, East plays the two and South the
four. West continues with the king of hearts, East playing the
seven and South the queen. How should West plan the defence?

36. Love all; dealer North.   Contract: 4S by South.

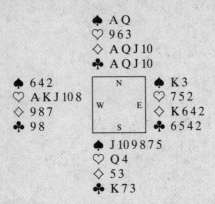

         ♠ A Q
         ♡ 9 6 3
         ◇ A Q J 10
         ♣ A Q J 10

♠ 6 4 2   ♠ K 3
♡ A K J 10 8   ♡ 7 5 2
◇ 9 8 7   ◇ K 6 4 2
♣ 9 8   ♣ 6 5 4 2

         ♠ J 10 9 8 7 5
         ♡ Q 4
         ◇ 5 3
         ♣ K 7 3

The defence
West should ask himself, 'Where is the ♡5?' East would have
petered with a doubleton, so clearly he holds the ♡5 and is
trying to convey a subtle message. He wants a diamond switch,
not a club. As we have seen, the higher card suggests an interest
in the higher-ranking suit. With the ♣K, instead of the ◇K,
East would have played the ♡5 on the second round. These
small clues can be vital. The diamond switch at trick three leaves
the declarer helpless. On a club switch South must reject the
spade finesse. The ♠A is followed by the ♠Q, and now, with
the trump suit unblocked, there are no further problems.

The principle
Defenders have many chances to help one another by intelligent
signalling. In the above hand West must divine which minor suit
to attack after he has cashed his heart winners. Without East's
assistance it would be a guess.

37. Game all; dealer South.   Contract: 4H by South.

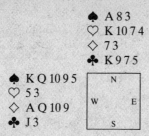

♠ A 8 3
♥ K 10 7 4
♦ 7 3
♣ K 9 7 5

♠ K Q 10 9 5
♥ 5 3
♦ A Q 10 9
♣ J 3

The bidding

S	W	N	E
1♥	1♠	3♥	Pass
4♥	Pass	Pass	Pass

West leads the king of spades and is allowed to hold the trick,
East following with the two. The spade continuation is won in
dummy and a third round ruffed by declarer. The trumps are
drawn in two rounds ending in dummy (East follows with the six
and knave). Declarer then tackles the diamond suit, this trick
comprising the three from dummy, the two from East and the
knave from declarer – West winning with the queen. Now the
ace of diamonds is cashed, declarer following with the king. How
should West continue?

37. Game all; dealer South.   Contract 4H by South.

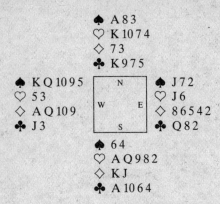

♠ A 8 3
♡ K 10 7 4
♢ 7 3
♣ K 9 7 5

♠ K Q 10 9 5   ♠ J 7 2
♡ 5 3   ♡ J 6
♢ A Q 10 9   ♢ 8 6 5 4 2
♣ J 3   ♣ Q 8 2

♠ 6 4
♡ A Q 9 8 2
♢ K J
♣ A 10 6 4

The defence
It is clear that declarer started with a 2-5-2-4 distribution; thus
West must continue with a spade or a diamond, but not a club.
The resulting ruff and discard will not resolve declarer's problem
(the avoidance of a club loser) whereas a club switch could. For
example the knave may be won in dummy; East's queen can then
be picked up with a simple finesse. A small club from West won't
improve the defence. First East's queen will be captured, then
West's knave will fall on the next round.

The principle
When you know that a critical side suit is divided 4-4 it is often
correct to concede a ruff and discard in preference to opening up
the danger suit. When declarer holds A10xx opposite K9xx there
is no immediate benefit from a discard. Even if the side suit is
stronger, for example AJxx opposite K10xx, a ruff and discard
does not solve declarer's problem – the position of the queen.

38. E-W game; dealer South.   Contract: 3NT by South.

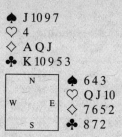

♠ J 10 9 7
♡ 4
♢ A Q J
♣ K 10 9 5 3

♠ 6 4 3
♡ Q J 10
♢ 7 6 5 2
♣ 8 7 2

The bidding

S	N
1NT*	2♣
2♡	2NT
3NT	

(*12–14 points)

West leads the five of hearts to East's ten and South's three.
How should East plan the defence?

Returning the right card

38. E-W game; dealer South.   Contract: 3NT by South.

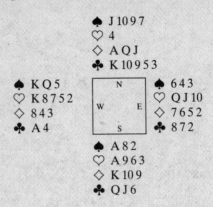

```
                    ♠ J 10 9 7
                    ♡ 4
                    ◇ A Q J
                    ♣ K 10 9 5 3
   ♠ K Q 5          ┌─────────┐      ♠ 6 4 3
   ♡ K 8 7 5 2      │    N    │      ♡ Q J 10
   ◇ 8 4 3          │ W     E │      ◇ 7 6 5 2
   ♣ A 4            │    S    │      ♣ 8 7 2
                    └─────────┘
                    ♠ A 8 2
                    ♡ A 9 6 3
                    ◇ K 10 9
                    ♣ Q J 6
```

The defence
East should return the ♡J at trick two, not the ♡Q. The point is
that the ♡Q will make it clear that East must have started with
♡QJ10, enabling declarer to go up with the ace and block the
suit. When the ♡J is returned, however, declarer may duck
again, hoping that East holds the ♣A and that communication
to the winning hearts has been broken.

The principle
Playing cards automatically is a bad habit. In the above example
it may seem natural to return the ♡Q at trick two, but closer
study reveals the advantage of playing the ♡J. It is a sound
principle to mislead the declarer when there is no danger that
partner will also be misled.

39. E-W game; dealer West.   Contract: 6S by South.

♠ J86
♡ AKJ75
♢ J
♣ A853

	N		♠ 9743
W		E	♡ Q1082
	S		♢ Q
			♣ J974

The bidding

S	W	N	E
—	3◇	Double	Pass
5♠	Pass	6♠	Pass
Pass	Pass		

West leads the ace of diamonds and continues with the king
when East follows with the queen. Dummy ruffs the second trick
with the knave of spades. How should East plan the defence?

39. E-W game; dealer West.   Contract: 6S by South.

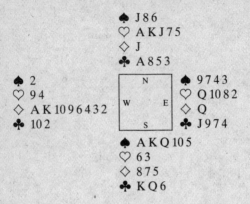

♠ J 8 6
♡ A K J 7 5
◇ J
♣ A 8 5 3

♠ 2
♡ 9 4
◇ A K 10 9 6 4 3 2
♣ 10 2

♠ 9 7 4 3
♡ Q 10 8 2
◇ Q
♣ J 9 7 4

♠ A K Q 10 5
♡ 6 3
◇ 8 7 5
♣ K Q 6

The defence
East cannot spare either a heart or a club (the former would enable declarer to ruff the suit good and the latter would establish dummy's fourth club), so he must underruff. This will not assist the declarer, and since he cannot safely ruff his third diamond in dummy he will have to look to the clubs or hearts for his twelfth trick. As neither suit breaks and the menace cards are misplaced for a squeeze, the contract must fail.

The principle
A friend once remarked, 'In our circle we ruff and we overruff, and we may even crossruff, but we have our principles – we never underruff.' An admirable code for the *Woosters*. As we have just seen, there are indeed moments when it is correct to underruff, most commonly when a player holds vital cards in the side suits that he cannnot spare. In such a setting a small trump has no more value than a penny in a foreign land.

40. Love all; dealer South.   Contract: 6H by South.

♠ A K 6 4
♡ Q 10 9 7 5
♢ 8
♣ A 3 2

```
        N       ♠ 8 3 2
                ♡ 3 2
    W       E   ♢ A 7 4 3
        S       ♣ Q 8 7 6
```

The bidding

S	N
1♡	2♠
3♡	4♣
4♢	4♡
5♡	6♡

Ambitious bidding took N-S dangerously high – but will they make the contract? West leads the knave of diamonds. How should East plan the defence?

40. Love all; dealer South.   Contract: 6H by South.

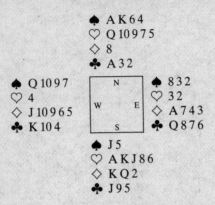

                    ♠ A K 6 4
                    ♡ Q 10 9 7 5
                    ♢ 8
                    ♣ A 3 2
    ♠ Q 10 9 7   ♠ 8 3 2
    ♡ 4   N   ♡ 3 2
    ♢ J 10 9 6 5   W   E   ♢ A 7 4 3
    ♣ K 10 4   S   ♣ Q 8 7 6
                    ♠ J 5
                    ♡ A K J 8 6
                    ♢ K Q 2
                    ♣ J 9 5

The defence

East should duck the diamond. The lead and the bidding make it
clear that South has the ♢KQ. If he has a small one as well the ace
will be a disastrous card for East to play, allowing declarer to
discard both dummy's club losers. By withholding the ♢A East
will lose this trick, but his side will gain *two* club tricks instead.
That is handsome compensation for West's failure to find the
killing club lead.

The principle

One needs courage to withhold an ace in a slam when there is a
singleton in dummy, but if it is a question of losing one trick in
order to gain two the terms are sufficiently attractive. A review of
North's aggressive bidding should indicate that declarer will have
nothing in reserve.

41. Game all; dealer North.   Contract: 3NT by South.

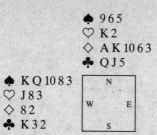

```
              ♠ 9 6 5
              ♡ K 2
              ◇ A K 10 6 3
              ♣ Q J 5
  ♠ K Q 10 8 3    ┌──────────┐
  ♡ J 8 3         │    N     │
  ◇ 8 2           │ W     E  │
  ♣ K 3 2         │    S     │
                  └──────────┘
```

The bidding

N	S
1◇	2♣
2◇	2♡
3♣	3NT

West leads the king of spades, dummy plays the five, East the two and South the ace. Declarer enters dummy with a diamond and plays the queen of clubs losing to West's king. How should West plan the defence?

Trust partner's card

41. Game all; dealer North.   Contract: 3NT by South.

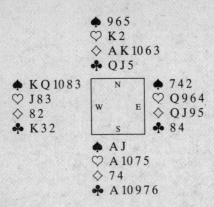

```
                    ♠ 9 6 5
                    ♡ K 2
                    ◇ A K 10 6 3
                    ♣ Q J 5
    ♠ K Q 10 8 3     ┌─────────┐      ♠ 7 4 2
    ♡ J 8 3          │    N    │      ♡ Q 9 6 4
    ◇ 8 2            │ W     E │      ◇ Q J 9 5
    ♣ K 3 2          │    S    │      ♣ 8 4
                     └─────────┘
                    ♠ A J
                    ♡ A 10 7 5
                    ◇ 7 4
                    ♣ A 10 9 7 6
```

The defence

West should cash the ♠Q, dropping South's knave, and run his spades to defeat the contract by one trick. Apart from the bidding and early play, there are several signposts that should direct West along the right road. East's ♠2 shows an odd number which can only be three. If East held the ♠J he would throw it on the first trick. If South held ♠AJx he would probably duck the first trick (Bath coup). All the evidence points to South holding the ♠AJ alone.

The principle

When uncertain of the distribution of a key suit pay special attention to partner's card. He will usually do his best to signal length. Taken in conjunction with the bidding and declarer's play it will normally be enough to complete the picture. On the above hand, declarer would have withheld his ace with Ax or Axx. With AJx it is usual to duck the first round although in the example hand it would not be essential. Exchange the ♣A for the ♣K and it would be mandatory. Conventionally, if East has the ♠J he must throw it on the lead of the king. This understanding saves West from having to guess.

42. E-W game; dealer South.   Contract: 4S by South.

♠ K 6
♡ A K Q 9 6 2
◇ Q 7
♣ A Q 10

        ♠ A Q
        ♡ 7 5 4
        ◇ 10 6 4 3 2
        ♣ K 9 2

The bidding

S	N
Pass	2NT
4♣	

West cashes the ace and king of diamonds, South following with
the eight and the knave. West now switches to the eight of clubs
which appears to be the top of a trebleton. East's king of clubs
wins the third trick and it is now obvious that the contract is going
to fail by at least two tricks, but how should East plan to extract
the maximum?

Ruff and discard and trump promotion

42. E-W game; dealer South.   Contract: 4S by South.

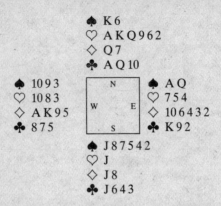

♠ K 6
♡ A K Q 9 6 2
♢ Q 7
♣ A Q 10

♠ 10 9 3   ♠ A Q
♡ 10 8 3   ♡ 7 5 4
♢ A K 9 5   ♢ 10 6 4 3 2
♣ 8 7 5   ♣ K 9 2

♠ J 8 7 5 4 2
♡ J
♢ J 8
♣ J 6 4 3

The defence
East should play a third round of diamonds, giving declarer a ruff
and discard. Furthermore, he should continue diamonds each
time he is on lead with a spade. When the fifth diamond is played
West's ♣10 will be promoted and the contract will fail by *three*
tricks. This was the defence found by Sharyn Kokish and Diana
Gordon in the 1982 world pairs championships in Biarritz.

The principle
When you have cashed all your side winners it is invariably correct
to try to weaken declarer's trump holding by continuing your long
suit. The ruff and discards that you concede will not provide any
extra tricks for the declarer, as he has plenty of winners anyway.
But his trump holding may well suffer so that the defenders either
gain control or obtain a promotion.

43 E-W game; dealer South.   Contract: 4H by South.

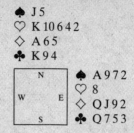

♠ J 5
♡ K 10 6 4 2
♢ A 6 5
♣ K 9 4

♠ A 9 7 2
♡ 8
♢ Q J 9 2
♣ Q 7 5 3

The bidding

S	N
1♡	4♡

West leads the king of spades and continues the suit to East's ace.
East switches to the eight of hearts. South draws trumps in two
rounds and then plays the ace, king and another diamond,
everyone following. East in now on lead – how should he plan the
defence?

43 E-W game; dealer South.   Contract 4H by South.

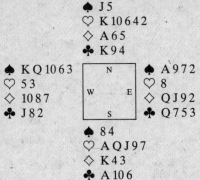

```
                        ♠ J 5
                        ♡ K 10 6 4 2
                        ◊ A 6 5
                        ♣ K 9 4
  ♠ K Q 10 6 3                        ♠ A 9 7 2
  ♡ 5 3                               ♡ 8
  ◊ 10 8 7                            ◊ Q J 9 2
  ♣ J 8 2                             ♣ Q 7 5 3
                        ♠ 8 4
                        ♡ A Q J 9 7
                        ◊ K 4 3
                        ♣ A 10 6
```

The defence

East is caught in an elimination end-play and must exit with a club (anything else would present declarer with a ruff and discard – and his contract), but it is important that he plays his honour – yes, the queen – so that declarer has a guess. The point is that with QJxx East might also play the queen. Should East play a small club South will run it round to dummy, picking up West's knave, and then finesse against East's queen on the way back. The critical card that guides East's play is the ♣9. With that card in dummy, and partner marked with three cards in the suit, there is absolutely no case for exiting with a low club.

The principle

When caught in an end-play it is important whenever possible to exit with a card that gives declarer a guess. In the above example, the declarer should still succeed after the lead of the ♣Q by winning with the ♣A then finessing dummy's nine. (Note that if East had the ♣QJxx he should at least *contemplate* unblocking in diamonds.) Interchange the ♣9 and ♣10 and East has to make an important decision. The ♣10 is now on view, but who holds the ♣9? If East guesses that it is his partner, J92 instead of J82, then a small club is right. But if he judges that it is with declarer, then the queen offers the defence the only realistic chance.

44 Love all; dealer South.   Contract: 6NT by South.

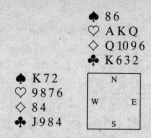

♠ 86
♡ A K Q
♢ Q 10 9 6
♣ K 6 3 2

♠ K 7 2
♡ 9 8 7 6
♢ 8 4
♣ J 9 8 4

The bidding

S	N
2NT	6NT

West leads the nine of hearts to dummy's queen, East's two and South's four. The declarer cashes four rounds of diamonds and West is forced to make two discards. What should they be?

Anticipating the end-play

44 Love all; dealer South.   Contract: 6NT by South.

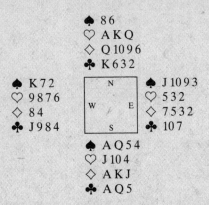

```
              ♠ 86
              ♡ A K Q
              ◇ Q 10 9 6
              ♣ K 6 3 2
  ♠ K 7 2                    ♠ J 10 9 3
  ♡ 9 8 7 6          N       ♡ 5 3 2
  ◇ 8 4         W        E   ◇ 7 5 3 2
  ♣ J 9 8 4          S       ♣ 10 7
              ♠ A Q 5 4
              ♡ J 10 4
              ◇ A K J
              ♣ A Q 5
```

The defence

West should discard his two small spades, baring the king. It would be fatal to throw a club, and futile to throw one spade and one heart because declarer would simply cash his winners in the red suits and then play four rounds of clubs, leaving West to play away from ♠Kx.

The principle

When you envisage an end-play it pays to plan ahead. If necessary, bare an honour card early in the play. The apparent risk is often a delusion. Far worse is to pin-point the position for declarer by huddling at the critical moment, or lamely allow yourself to be end-played.

45 Game all; dealer North.   Contract: 3NT by South.

```
              ♠ 842
              ♡ A K
              ◇ Q 7
              ♣ A J 9 8 6 5
                              ♠ 65
                              ♡ J 8 7 5
                              ◇ K J 4
                              ♣ K 4 3 2
```

The bidding

N	S
1♣	1♡
2♣	3NT

West leads the knave of spades which South wins with the king.
South now plays the queen of clubs which East ducks. South
continues with the ten of clubs overtaking with dummy's knave
while West discards the three of spades. How should East plan the
defence?

Switching with the right card

45 Game all; dealer North.   Contract: 3NT by South.

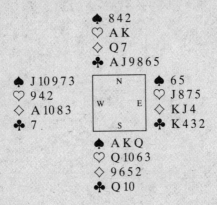

```
              ♠ 8 4 2
              ♡ A K
              ♢ Q 7
              ♣ A J 9 8 6 5

  ♠ J 10 9 7 3      N        ♠ 6 5
  ♡ 9 4 2                    ♡ J 8 7 5
  ♢ A 10 8 3   W       E     ♢ K J 4
  ♣ 7              S         ♣ K 4 3 2

              ♠ A K Q
              ♡ Q 10 6 3
              ♢ 9 6 5 2
              ♣ Q 10
```

The defence
East should win with the ♣K and switch to the ♢J. West's spade
discard suggests that he started with a spade suit headed by the
J 109 (it could have been A J 109). If the contract is to be defeated
West will have to hold four diamonds at least as good as A 108x.
East must lead the *knave* otherwise the suit will be blocked on the
third round.

The principle
Sometimes it is easy to find the right switch, not always so easy to
choose the right card. When partner indicates that his original suit
should be abandoned, or when this inference can reasonably be
drawn, there are two factors to consider before changing direction
– the suit and the card. In the example hand diamonds are
obviously declarer's only possible weakness. Since four tricks are
required East must ensure there is no blockage. If East foresees
that possibility then the knave must be the right card to play. Note
the fine collaboration between East and West: East ducks the first
club, which gives West the opportunity to discard a spade. That
discard carries an unmistakable message.

46 Love all; dealer East.   Contract: 3NT by South.

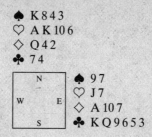

♠ K 8 4 3
♡ A K 10 6
◇ Q 4 2
♣ 7 4

♠ 9 7
♡ J 7
◇ A 10 7
♣ K Q 9 6 5 3

The bidding

S	W	N	E
—	—	—	Pass
1NT*	Pass	2♣	Double
2◇	Pass	3NT	Pass
Pass	Pass		

(*12–14 points)

Playing MUD leads, West starts with the eight of clubs in response to his partner's double. How should East play to this trick, and how should he plan the defence when declarer leads a small diamond to the queen?

46 Love all; dealer East.   Contract: 3NT by South.

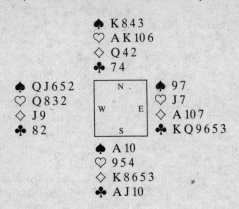

♠ K 8 4 3
♡ A K 10 6
◇ Q 4 2
♣ 7 4

♠ Q J 6 5 2   ♠ 9 7
♡ Q 8 3 2   ♡ J 7
◇ J 9   ◇ A 10 7
♣ 8 2   ♣ K Q 9 6 5 3

♠ A 10
♡ 9 5 4
◇ K 8 6 5 3
♣ A J 10

The defence
East should play low to the opening club lead in order to preserve the communications. When South plays a small diamond to the queen, East should disinterestedly follow with the seven. Declarer will probably continue diamonds and when East follows with the ten he will duck in hand, hoping that West has the bare ace (coup en blanc). West wins the second round of diamonds and plays his last club. East can now clear the club suit and must eventually regain the lead to cash his winners. The defence make two diamonds and three clubs.

The principle
There is a double principle involved on this hand. **1** In order to keep the communications intact, it is often correct to allow declarer to win a cheap trick on the first round of the suit. If partner regains the lead he can continue and clear the suit. **2** By unemotionally withholding your ace in the suit declarer attacks (in the above case, diamonds), you may persuade him that his best chance is to play your partner for Ax. This enables you to retain your card of entry while partner's entry helps to clear your suit.

47 Game all; dealer South.   Contract: 4H by South.

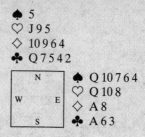

♠ 5
♡ J 9 5
◇ 10 9 6 4
♣ Q 7 5 4 2

                    ♠ Q 10 7 6 4
                    ♡ Q 10 8
                    ◇ A 8
                    ♣ A 6 3

The bidding

S	N
2♠	2NT
3♡	4♡
No	

West leads the knave of clubs, dummy plays low, East puts on the ace and South follows with the king. East now cashes the ace of diamonds, South following with the queen and West the two. How should East plan the defence?

Sacrificing an honour in a good cause

47 Game all; dealer South.   Contract: 4H by South.

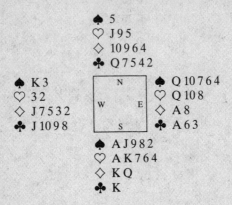

```
                    ♠ 5
                    ♡ J 9 5
                    ◇ 10 9 6 4
                    ♣ Q 7 5 4 2
    ♠ K 3              N           ♠ Q 10 7 6 4
    ♡ 3 2                          ♡ Q 10 8
    ◇ J 7 5 3 2   W       E        ◇ A 8
    ♣ J 10 9 8        S            ♣ A 6 3
                    ♠ A J 9 8 2
                    ♡ A K 7 6 4
                    ◇ K Q
                    ♣ K
```

The defence

Although West obviously didn't appreciate it when he was on
lead, it is clear that the right defensive game is to play trumps
(East only cashed the ◇A in case a losing diamond was discarded
on the ♣Q): but a low trump is not good enough. East must play
the ♡Q at trick three. Note the difference: when a low trump is
played, declarer wins with dummy's nine and has no trouble in
trumping two spades. The ♠9 is discarded on the ♣Q. Subsequently trumps are drawn and he concedes just one more trick –
the ♠J. When the queen of trumps is returned, declarer has to win
in his own hand and use the ♡J9 for ruffing the spades. That
leaves him with the same losing spade *plus* a losing trump.

The principle

When it is right to attack trumps it sometimes pays to play an
honour rather than a small one. When this play forces declarer to
win with a high honour in his own hand and ruff with high
intermediates in dummy the gambit may be especially potent. As
in the above hand, the trick often returns with a dividend.

48 Game all; dealer South.   Contract: 4S by South.

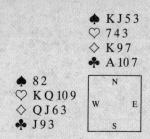

♠ K J 5 3
♡ 7 4 3
◇ K 9 7
♣ A 10 7

♠ 8 2
♡ K Q 10 9
◇ Q J 6 3
♣ J 9 3

The bidding

S	N
1♠	3♠
4♠	

West leads the king of hearts and continues the suit when his
partner encourages with the eight. South ruffs the third heart,
draws two rounds of trumps and then plays the ace, king and
another diamond. Everyone follows to the diamonds and West is
now on lead; how should he plan the defence?

48 Game all; dealer South.   Contract: 4S by South.

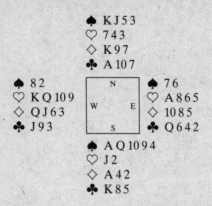

♠ K J 5 3
♡ 7 4 3
♦ K 9 7
♣ A 10 7

♠ 8 2
♡ K Q 10 9
♦ Q J 6 3
♣ J 9 3

♠ 7 6
♡ A 8 6 5
♦ 10 8 5
♣ Q 6 4 2

♠ A Q 10 9 4
♡ J 2
♦ A 4 2
♣ K 8 5

The defence
West is caught in an elimination end-play. If he exits with a red suit the ruff and discard sees declarer home. So West must play a club, and with the ♣10 visible in dummy he must specifically play the ♣J – the only card that ensures defeat of the contract (had East been on play in this position the winning defence would have been a low club – not the queen). Here, as is often the case, the critical cards are the nine and ten. The key question is who holds them? If West makes the mistake of playing a low club, declarer can play low from dummy, capture East's queen and then finesse the ten on the next round.

The principle
It is often the right counter to an elimination and throw-in for a defender to exit with an honour card rather than one of the small ones. When you hold the nine as well (J9x or Q9x) and dummy holds A 10 x (K 10 x), it is mandatory to play your honour when under the dummy and a low card when over the dummy.

49 Game all; dealer West.   Contract: 4S by South.

♠ 8752
♡ A J 4
♢ A J 10
♣ A K Q

♠ A K 3
♡ K Q 10 6
♢ Q 9 7 5 3 2
♣ –

	N	
W		E
	S	

The bidding

S	W	N	E
—	1♢	Double	2♢
2♠	3♡	3NT	Pass
4♠	Pass	Pass	Pass

West leads the king of hearts. Declarer wins in dummy, East playing the three and South the two. A spade to the king, East discarding a small club, gives West the lead once more. How should he plan the defence?

Forcing an entry

49 Game all; dealer West.   Contract: 4S by South.

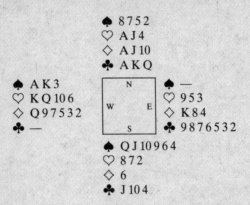

```
                    ♠ 8 7 5 2
                    ♡ A J 4
                    ♢ A J 10
                    ♣ A K Q
    ♠ A K 3              N              ♠ —
    ♡ K Q 10 6                          ♡ 9 5 3
    ♢ Q 9 7 5 3 2    W       E          ♢ K 8 4
    ♣ —                  S              ♣ 9 8 7 6 5 3 2
                    ♠ Q J 10 9 6 4
                    ♡ 8 7 2
                    ♢ 6
                    ♣ J 10 4
```

The defence

Mrs Jane Priday, former world champion, was the original West
on this hand and she rose to the occasion with the brilliant
continuation of the ♡10 at trick three. Dummy had to win with
the knave, but when a second trump was played Jane won and
played the ♡6 to her partner's nine. East returned a club for the
ruff that spelt one down. No other defence will succeed. Perhaps it
is worth noting that the declarer would have done better to have
ducked the opening lead. But sometimes defenders can only play
as well as declarer permits.

The principle

When you desperately need to put partner on play, consider if
there is any card he might hold which will give him an eventual
entry. Even if your play entails the risk of conceding an extra
trick, the reward often makes the gamble well worth while.

50 E-W game; dealer South.   Contract: 6H by South.

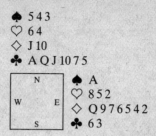

♠ 5 4 3
♡ 6 4
♢ J 10
♣ A Q J 10 7 5

N

W　E

S

♠ A
♡ 8 5 2
♢ Q 9 7 6 5 4 2
♣ 6 3

The bidding

S	N
2♡	3♣
3♡	4♡
4NT	5♢
6♡	

Aggressive bidding led to an ambitious contract – but will it be defeated after the lead of the queen of spades? How should East plan the defence?

Defence against a squeeze

50 E-W game; dealer South. Contract: 6H by South.

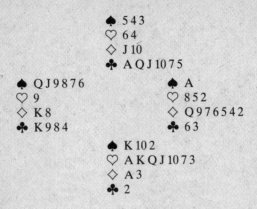

```
                    ♠ 5 4 3
                    ♡ 6 4
                    ◇ J 10
                    ♣ A Q J 10 7 5
  ♠ Q J 9 8 7 6                    ♠ A
  ♡ 9                              ♡ 8 5 2
  ◇ K 8                            ◇ Q 9 7 6 5 4 2
  ♣ K 9 8 4                        ♣ 6 3
                    ♠ K 10 2
                    ♡ A K Q J 10 7 3
                    ◇ A 3
                    ♣ 2
```

The defence

East should return a club at trick two! Declarer will win a cheap trick with dummy's ten, but not his contract. Suppose for example East returns a diamond, South can win the ◇A and cash all the heart winners and the ♠K. Before the last heart is played everyone is down to four cards, and West will have to find a discard from ♠J and ♣K98. If he lets go the spade, declarer's ten becomes good and the simple club finesse yields the extra trick. If West parts with a club, dummy's ♣AQJ, with the aid of the finesse, will provide the last three tricks.

The principle

In order for a squeeze to work there must be a link with a long menace (two or more cards in a suit with at least one card of master rank; in this case clubs). If the link is broken the squeeze fails. Thus, when threatened by a squeeze, the defence must seek to destroy the communications. In the above hand, East could not be sure that South held a singleton club (with a doubleton the contract would be cold anyway), but if he did it was vital to attack the suit.

51 Love all; dealer South.   Contract: 3NT by South.

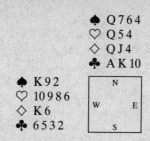

♠ Q 7 6 4
♥ Q 5 4
♦ Q J 4
♣ A K 10

♠ K 9 2
♥ 10 9 8 6
♦ K 6
♣ 6 5 3 2

The bidding

S	N
1♦	1♠
1NT*	3NT

(*Showing 15–16 points)

West leads the ten of hearts which is won by dummy's queen, East following with the two and South the knave. The queen of diamonds now loses to West's king, East contributing the two and South the three. How should West plan the defence?

51 Love all; dealer South.   Contract: 3NT by South.

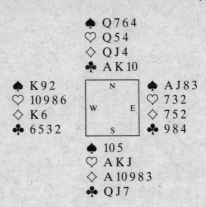

```
              ♠ Q764
              ♡ Q54
              ◇ QJ4
              ♣ AK10
  ♠ K92         N        ♠ AJ83
  ♡ 10986              ♡ 732
  ◇ K6      W      E    ◇ 752
  ♣ 6532        S        ♣ 984
              ♠ 105
              ♡ AKJ
              ◇ A10983
              ♣ QJ7
```

The defence

West should switch to the ♠9. It is clear that the defence must look to the spade suit for tricks, but it is not good enough for West to lead any spade. It must be precisely the nine. If, for example, West leads the ♠2 East will win with the ♠J and return the ♠3 to West's king. But now if declarer refuses to cover the ♠9 blocks the suit.

The principle

If you need a suit to provide a given number of tricks you must direct your mind to a possible distribution that will fulfil your requirements. Sometimes you must select the right *card* to avoid a subsequent blockage.

52 Love all; dealer East.   Contract: 4S by South.

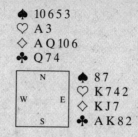

♠ 10 6 5 3
♡ A 3
♢ A Q 10 6
♣ Q 7 4

```
        N
              ♠ 8 7
   W      E   ♡ K 7 4 2
              ♢ K J 7
        S     ♣ A K 8 2
```

The bidding

S	W	N	E
—	—	—	1NT
2♠	Pass	4♠	Pass
Pass	Pass	Pass	

West leads the knave of clubs. Declarer ducks the first round but covers the ten with the queen. East wins the second trick with the king of clubs and tries the ace, which South ruffs. Trumps are drawn in two rounds, both defenders following. Now the nine of diamonds is run to East's knave. How should East continue?

Counting up to thirteen

52 Love all; dealer East.   Contract: 4S by South.

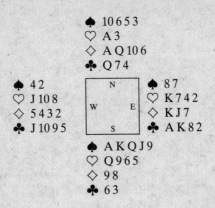

```
                    ♠ 10 6 5 3
                    ♡ A 3
                    ♢ A Q 10 6
                    ♣ Q 7 4
    ♠ 4 2              N          ♠ 8 7
    ♡ J 10 8      W       E       ♡ K 7 4 2
    ♢ 5 4 3 2                     ♢ K J 7
    ♣ J 10 9 5       S            ♣ A K 8 2
                    ♠ A K Q J 9
                    ♡ Q 9 6 5
                    ♢ 9 8
                    ♣ 6 3
```

The defence

East should play a diamond straight back into dummy's A Q 10.
Declarer can enjoy his diamond tricks, and one discard, but
cannot avoid losing a heart trick for one down. If East errs by
playing a heart, South can make his contract with the loss of only
one diamond and two clubs. The clue to the correct defence on
this hand is counting. South has shown seven black cards (two
clubs known and five spades inferred), thus he must hold six red
cards. So unless declarer has a five-card diamond suit – which is
unlikely – the discards, if any, will be useless to him.

The principle

The solution to East's problem is often provided by counting. If
the total cards held in two suits are known it is not difficult to work
out the balance held in the other two suits. Then a moment's
thought will usually be enough to decide the correct defence. If
the count in two suits is not complete you may have to rely on
inferences, both negative and positive, that you can draw from the
bidding.

Gyles Brandreth
Solo Games £1.95

Master gamester Gyles Brandreth has come up with a unique
compendium of ways to pit your wits against yourself. All the well-
known favourites – patience, solitaire, darts – plus lots of new ones to
try. Choose from the cerebral and challenging or the simple and fun. The
ideal way of whiling away a rainy day or a long journey.

Basil Dalton
The Complete Patience Book £1.75

You may be alone . . . but you'll never be lonely when you discover the
pleasure of patience. You'll find hours of absorbing but relaxing activity
in this complete guide to a fascinating pastime . . . An authority on card
games, the late Basil Dalton was an expert on Patience. Here, in one
volume, are the results of his years of interest in the subject. Some are
easy, some are more difficult – all provide a unique form of mental
exercise and entertainment.

edited by Mike Grimshaw
**The Second Pan Book of
Jumbo Crosswords** £1.50

The Pan Book of Crosswords series has been called the best puzzle
book series ever. Now, in this follow-up to the successful *Pan Book of
Jumbo Crosswords*, series editor Mike Grimshaw has come up with
another fifty brand-new puzzles. A feast of puzzlement guaranteed to
delight every crossword addict.

Waddingtons Illustrated Card Games £3.95

An essential reference book for every card player, a treasure trove for family evenings. Here are the rules, procedures and techniques for more than 200 games – patience games, memory games, gambling games, from the simplest forms of snap to the intricacies of bridge and canasta.

Hubert Phillips
The Pan Book of Card Games £1.95

No other book of card games explains so many games so thoroughly or offers so much instruction. The late Hubert Phillips, first chairman of the English Bridge Union, was long recognized as Britain's leading authority on card games. This famous work, with its clear descriptions and its innumerable specimen hands played out card by card, will afford every reader hours of entertainment.

'This fine book describes all the best of the old games and several new ones' OBSERVER

'Hubert Phillips describes most lucidly fifty card games and more than twenty-five games of Patience' SUNDAY TIMES

Robert Harbin
Waddingtons Family Card Games £1.50

A pack of cards can give more fun than anything else; it is an endless source of enjoyment. In his book, Robert Harbin demonstrates this as he entertainingly and clearly describes more than sixty card games, from traditional ones like Whist, Solo and Bridge, to the lesser known and even rare games such as Pishti, Cloboish and Solomon.

Waddingtons Illustrated Encyclopaedia of Games £4.95

This complete compendium of board games, dice games, party games, target games and many more has something for everyone. From spoof to musical chairs, conkers to tiddleywinks, ludo to backgammon, here are the rules and instructions for over 300 old and new, easy and difficult, familiar and unusual games. Beautifully illustrated throughout, this book is the ideal party companion and an essential for every family bookshelf.

Gerald Abrahams
The Pan Book of Chess £1.95

Starting – for the benefit of the complete tyro – with the basic moves and rules of chess, the author goes on to describe the subtle features of the game. The book initiates the beginner into methods of exploiting the 'fork', the 'pin', etc, demonstrates tactics and strategy, shows how battles are won – or lost – and examines and analyses openings and endgames. Throughout, the author illustrates his lessons with examples from actual play, including many brilliant games by the masters.

Jeremy Flint and John Gullick
The First Bridge Book £2.50

The authors have pooled their enormous experience of bridge, and of teaching the game, to produce this invaluable guide for absolute beginners, as well as those who already play but would welcome a refresher course. All the rules, conventions and terms are explained here, systematically and sensibly, for the newcomer to this aristocrat of card games. Above all, every page insists that bridge is fun!

Freddie North and Jeremy Flint
Bridge: the first principles £2.50

Because they have so much to absorb, beginners at bridge invariably
become preoccupied with the scoring, the order of suits, the elements
of bidding and so on. No matter how talented and patient bridge writers
and teachers may be, many of their students still find difficulty with
even the rudiments of card play. In this book the authors have combined
their long experience to produce the perfect antidote, taking the reader
gently from the most elementary concepts to an all round grasp of the
subject. *Bridge: the first principles* will prove an invaluable guide.